IN SEARCH OF *Shalom*

Praises for
IN SEARCH OF SHALOM

"Great Biblical insights, great practical life applications for men of all ages! If you are serious about changing your direction this is your handbook."

~ ALLEN HUTH, Vice President of Gideons International

"Working in a professional sport for the past 20 years, the internal and external pressures to find or create one's own success is an oppressive force. It wounds and destroys so many of the men that I serve and their families I have worked with and observed. Some fond "success" as defined by the world but few find peace, God's shalom. No matter the height of success, without God they cannot account for the emptiness they feel inside. The Psalms are a balm, a slave for the hurting heart. Hanschke, here, aptly applies their healing aid to the one who is spiritually hurting, spiritually hungry, spiritually searching. His book will wonderfully shepherd one who longs to leave Meshek and find a contented place in the house of the Lord. I encourage you to join him on this journey and let him be your guide."

~ REV. BRAD KENNEY, Chaplain, Colorado Rapids

"I have had the privilege of knowing Roy Hanschke for the past twenty years. This book exemplifies his passion and love for God, His Word and His people. I highly recommend this book for all men who desire to know real success, real peace… the way God intended it to be!"

~ LARRY ALBERTSON, Director, Leadership By The Book

IN
SEARCH
OF
Shalom

The Success Every Man Desires

A PILGRIMAGE THROUGH
PSALMS 120-134

ROY
HANSCHKE

NASHVILLE

LONDON • NEW YORK • MELBOURNE • VANCOUVER

IN SEARCH OF *Shalom*
The Success Every Man Desires || A Pilgrimage Through Psalms 120-134

Published in New York, New York, by Morgan James Publishing. Morgan James is a trademark of Morgan James, LLC. www.MorganJamesPublishing.com

The Morgan James Speakers Group can bring authors to your live event. For more information or to book an event visit The Morgan James Speakers Group at www.TheMorganJamesSpeakersGroup.com.

ISBN # 9781683507024 paperback
ISBN # 9781683507031 eBook
Library of Congress Control Number: 2017912051

Cover and Interior Design by:
Rachel Lopez
www.r2cdesign.com

In an effort to support local communities, raise awareness and funds, Morgan James Publishing donates a percentage of all book sales for the life of each book to Habitat for Humanity Peninsula and Greater Williamsburg.

Get involved today! Visit
www.MorganJamesBuilds.com

Contents

Preface

The Pilgrim Psalms (Psalms 120-134) grabbed my attention about four years ago during my early morning Bible study. I began digging into them with a passion. I read commentaries and books from present and past authors. I took copious notes and sought God for understanding. Then God made it clear to me that my notes were to become a book for men.

Why make this a book for men? For a long time I've followed a calling from God to reach out to other Christian men through prayer and speaking engagements. I love to see men grab onto practical biblical wisdom that leads to a better life. So it was natural for me to make this a book for Christian men.

What's different about this book, you may ask. The market is full of Christian books for men. There are also books written about the Pilgrim Psalms. However, I found no book that uniquely combines the messages of the Pilgrim Psalms with the needs of modern Christian men. Furthermore, I made this a short book, suitable for busy men.

We as men want to live fulfilling lives and experience success in all our efforts. Our problem is that we often go about it in ineffective ways. This book spells out God's ways.

I've learned a lot both from writing and reading this book. There have been occasions when I've stopped writing or reading and gotten on my knees to ask God to forgive me for doing things the wrong way.

I'm still growing. My pilgrimage isn't over. I still have much to learn and apply. My desire is that we as men can grow together as we take the pilgrimage in search of Shalom.

I hope this book will stimulate you to think. I hope you will share it with other men. In fact, I recommend that you read it and talk about it with another man (a son, father, or friend) or a group of men. I pray that it will change your life as it has mine.

I'd like to give special thanks to God, with whom I spent many hours, days, and months seeking the meaning and application of the Pilgrim Psalms.

Thanks to family and friends who encouraged me and gave me valuable feedback on early drafts.

Thanks to Morgan James Publishing for giving me the opportunity to get this message out to men.

Thanks to Angie Kiesling of The Editorial Attic for her great work and attention to my needs.

Introduction

This book is about a man, perhaps just like you. He believes in God and wants to be successful in all he does. Like most men, he sees himself as a provider and protector. He's made that way. He works hard to provide for himself and his family and he will fight to preserve what he has. He loves life and wants to experience all of it he can. He wants to bless and be blessed, to be fruitful and prosperous.

However, life doesn't always work out the way a man plans. The years pass by and he wonders if there is still time to experience many new things. Certain aspects about himself and the world bother him and he doesn't always like what's happening around him. He'd like to see some changes. He knows there's more to life and he wants to find it. He wants his life to work the way he believes it should work. Some days, he feels he should just give up and at other times he feels recharged and ready to push ahead. He may not realize it, but he's a man in search of Shalom.

Just what is Shalom? *Shalom* is a Hebrew word generally translated as "peace" in the Old Testament. However, it contains more than what you would normally think of as peace. It really means success the way God planned it. When asked what success means, many men will say success is having a great job, a lot of money, and status in his world. But those things fall far short of the Biblical concept of Shalom.

Dr. Aviezer Ravitzky[1] describes Shalom this way: "The Hebrew word for peace, Shalom, is derived from a root denoting wholeness or completeness, and its frame of reference throughout Jewish literature is bound up with the notion of *Shelemut*, perfection. Shalom is a blessing, a manifestation of divine grace." This shows that Shalom comes from one source. It comes from God. If a man is to find Shalom, he must find God.

This one word, "Shalom," actually incorporates the ideas of favor, prosperity, safety, well-being, tranquility, fullness, harmony within and without, restored relationships, and vigor and vitality in all dimensions of life. It's more than money can buy and more than fame can provide. It's the way things ought to be—the way God intended life to be. In Chapter 1, we'll see that the New Testament Greek word for peace carries the same meaning.

This book is intended to be a group study conducted by men. But, more than a study, it's a pilgrimage. I hope you will take the pilgrimage with other men and find restoration, refreshment, change, and renewal. May this journey rekindle the fire that once burned in you, but in a new way.

---

1   Dr. Aviezer Ravitzky is the Saul Rosenblum Chair of Jewish Philosophy and Chair of the Department of Jewish Thought at Hebrew University. He is the author of *Messianism, Zionism, and Jewish Religious Radicalism* and *History and Faith: Studies in Jewish Philosophy*. The quote was taken from www.myjewishlearning.com where it was reprinted with permission of The Gale Group from Contemporary Jewish Religious Thought, edited by Arthur A. Cohen and Paul Mendes-Flohr, Twayne Publishers.

Chapter 1

How Badly Do You Want Success in Life?

— PSALM 120 —

1 I call on the Lord in my distress, and he answers me.

2 Save me, Lord, from lying lips and from deceitful tongues.

3 What will he do to you, and what more besides, you deceitful tongue?

4 He will punish you with a warrior's sharp arrows, with burning coals of the broom bush.

5 Woe to me that I dwell in Meshek, that I live among the tents of Kedar!

6 Too long have I lived among those who hate peace.

7 I am for peace; but when I speak, they are for war.

Life was meant to be enjoyed, and all men want to feel successful. But how can we focus on such things when the world is changing so drastically and we can't seem to do anything about it? Every day, we're confronted with a changing moral climate, a struggling economy, political upheaval, the threat of terrorism, and a concern for our children and grandchildren who are bombarded with values different from ours. How can we bring some sense to our world, or stability to the chaos? How can we bring hope, peace, and contentment to our family? How can we live life to the full as God intended it?

Like the psalmist, maybe you're saying, "Too long have I lived in Meshek." You might be thinking, "I need to get away. I need to take a fresh look at my life and what it offers my family and the world around me." Psalm 120 establishes the need for a pilgrimage. It's a time to get away, rethink, and make some changes.

The man in Psalm 120 says he was tired of living in Meshek and Kedar. In Biblical times, Meshek was located north of Israel by the Black Sea. Kedar refers to nomads who wandered in the Arabian Desert southeast of Israel. These were places of hostility where peace was nearly impossible for the people of Israel. If an Israelite lived in either place, he would constantly feel the oppression of an argumentative, uncooperative, combative people. To say you lived in Meshek is to say you were living in an undesirable place. The psalmist had to get out of Meshek. He was ready for a change. He just wanted a little peace. Sound good?

He writes, "Too long have I lived among those who hate peace. I am for peace; but when I speak, they are for war." He wanted peace more than anything. What is this peace he's talking about? In the introduction, we defined the Hebrew word Shalom as "peace," but it actually incorporates all these concepts:

- Favor
- Prosperity
- Safety
- Well-being
- Tranquility
- Fullness
- Harmony within and without
- Restored relationships
- Vigor and vitality in all dimensions of life

Basically, it's the way things ought to be—the way God intended life to be. It's what a man wants for himself, his family, and his world. In a word, it's success, God's way. The New Testament concept of peace is similar. The Greek word for peace is *Eirene*. It carries the same meanings as Shalom. It stands for harmony, security, prosperity, and wholeness.

It also includes the idea of restored relationships. Perhaps some relationships in your life need restoring, but before you can do so with others, you first need to restore your relationship with God. Isaiah 59:2 says our sin has separated us from God. In order to restore the relationship, our sin problem has to be addressed. Jesus died to reconcile us, to bring us back into a relationship with God. As Romans 5:1 says, "Therefore, since we have been justified through faith, we have peace with God through our Lord Jesus Christ."

A restored relationship with God brings peace. When you believe that Christ died for you, you receive that peace, and things are made right between you and God. That's reconciliation. However, you may need to restore your relationship with God before you can fully restore relationships with others. That begins by accepting Jesus Christ and His death for you. Once a relationship with God is restored, you can restore your earthly relationships and experience all the other aspects of Shalom.

Throughout this study, we'll use the term "Meshek" to refer to the place where you live and work. The pilgrimage will take you away from Meshek, in mind and spirit, in order to realign your life with God so that you can experience His Shalom. Throughout this book, the word "Shalom" will always be capitalized. This is to remind you that Shalom comes from the presence of God.

By dwelling in Meshek too long, a man loses touch with the life characteristics of Shalom. How much have you lost by dwelling in Meshek? How much have you changed from the person you were or wanted to be? The purpose of this pilgrimage is for you to regain Shalom, perhaps in a way you never experienced it before. Whether you need to regain peace, experience it in a new way, or for the first time, Shalom is within your reach.

The pilgrim, in the days these psalms were collected as a unit, sought the literal City of Zion where God's temple resided. In essence, he sought the presence of God. He travelled with others and recited Psalm 120 through 134, one a day, until he reached his destination. It was in Jerusalem, at the journey's end, where he would experience the life-changing presence of God. Using these same psalms, your pilgrimage will take you to the very presence of God and allow you to experience Him in a new way. Your destination is the same as the writer of Psalm 84 who declares: "How lovely is your dwelling place, Lord Almighty! My soul yearns, even faints, for the courts of the Lord; my heart and my flesh cry out for the living God."

In the Old Testament Hebrew nation, when men embarked on their pilgrimages from Meshek to the City of Zion, they felt the freedom of getting away. However, the act of leaving Meshek didn't change them. Today, men sometimes leave their Meshek (their jobs and families) thinking that they can find a happier, more peaceful life, but their problems inevitably follow them. It's like taking a vacation only to return and find that you need another one.

What a man needs is a life-changing experience. He needs to change inwardly so that upon his return home he will face life differently and successfully. The intent of this pilgrimage is that you will change by having such an encounter with yourself and God. Throughout the rest of this book, you will deal with lessons God wants you to learn. Each one will bring you closer to experiencing Shalom. Your circumstances in Meshek are not going to change unless you change. Change isn't always easy, but the changes God brings in us reap fantastic rewards. So, ask yourself: how badly do you want success in life?

Consider the following New Testament verses that contain the word "peace" and discuss the questions below. Try to memorize one or more of the verses.

Peace I leave with you; my peace I give you. I do not give to you as the world gives. Do not let your hearts be troubled and do not be afraid. (**John 14:27**)

Finally, brothers and sisters, rejoice! Strive for full restoration, encourage one another, be of one mind, live in peace. And the God of love and peace will be with you. (**2 Corinthians 13:11**)

And the peace of God, which transcends all understanding, will guard your hearts and your minds in Christ Jesus. (**Philippians 4:7**)

No discipline seems pleasant at the time, but painful. Later on, however, it produces a harvest of righteousness and peace for those who have been trained by it. (**Hebrews 12:11**)

Peacemakers who sow in peace reap a harvest of righteousness. (**James 3:18**)

Now may the Lord of peace himself give you peace at all times and in every way. The Lord be with all of you. (**2 Thessalonians 3:16**)

Discussion:
1. What have you lost by dwelling in "Meshek"?
2. In the definition of peace presented in this chapter, several descriptive words were mentioned. Which word(s) grabbed your attention and why?
3. What relationships in your life need restoration?

4. Which New Testament passage or phrase is most meaningful to you and why?

5. What do you hope to gain by taking this pilgrimage?

Chapter 2

Who Is God to You?

— PSALM 121 —

1 I lift up my eyes to the mountains—where does my help come from?

2 My help comes from the Lord, the Maker of heaven and earth.

3 He will not let your foot slip—he who watches over you will not slumber;

4 indeed, he who watches over Israel will neither slumber nor sleep.

5 The Lord watches over you—the Lord is your shade at your right hand;

6 the sun will not harm you by day, nor the moon by night.

7 The Lord will keep you from all harm—he will watch over your life;

8 the Lord will watch over your coming and going both now and forevermore.

As you begin the pilgrimage in search of Shalom, there is both a warning and a word of encouragement to keep in mind. The warning is that this journey will not always be comfortable.

7

The search for Shalom requires an inward examination that will reveal things you need to change. But hang on. You're going to like the results. The changes are good and worth the discomfort. The encouragement is, "The Lord is your Keeper." No matter what happens to you on this journey, no matter what God tells you to do, keep this in mind: "The Lord is your Keeper." This is where you need to start.

We need help because the path we're traveling is slippery. We're going to face things about ourselves we may not like. We might slip and fall, but don't give up. Just get up and keep going. The temptation will be to go back to Meshek. You may think that however bad Meshek might be, it's home and you just want to make the best of it. There's a sense of security there, despite its faults.

When the children of Israel left Egypt, they experienced problems and wished they were back in Egypt where, at least, there was good food. Like the Israelites, you may at some point want to give up the journey and accept the lie that nothing is ever going to change. However, no matter how difficult the journey, you can courageously go on if you rest in the knowledge that the Lord is your keeper both now and forever. We'll look at what God does as your keeper, but first let's see who this God really is.

The psalmist calls God the Maker of heaven and earth who will not let your foot slip. He is your security. Is there any higher authority or greater, more knowledgeable help than the Maker of heaven and earth? Establish this fact now that God is your keeper. What does that mean? It doesn't mean that you will never encounter problems, failures, or heartaches. It doesn't mean that you will never face cancer, loss of a loved one, or never lose your source of income. However, in all these things God will be with you to keep your mind and soul from disaster.

"Keeper" is the translation of the Hebrew word *Shamar*. It's used several times in the psalm in the verb form translated as "to keep" or "watch." God is the one watching over you. Genesis 2:15 helps us understand the significance of this verb. There, we read, "The LORD God took the man and put him in the Garden of Eden to work it and take care of it." Adam was put in charge of the garden "to care for it." The word there is *Shamar*. Just as God assigned Adam to care for the garden, He has assigned Himself to care for you.

How does a good gardener care for his garden? He plants, nourishes, cultivates, and prunes it so he can accomplish his objective of having a fruitful harvest. That's what God does with you, His garden. He wants good results so He cares for you. He wants you to experience Shalom which is the success He has planned for you. Listen to Jesus' words about you in John 15:16: "You did not choose me, but I chose you and appointed you so that you might go and bear fruit, fruit that will last—and so that whatever you ask in my name the Father will give you." That's God's plan and purpose for you.

For example, I like to climb mountains, but the older I get the more uncertain I feel about jumping from rock to rock or skirting around narrow ledges. What if I knew for certain that I would never fall to my death while mountain climbing? What if I had a guarantee that, although I might slip and get a few bumps and bruises, I would always return safely? My fear of mountain climbing would change. I could courageously take to the trails no matter how difficult. That's the guarantee you have on this pilgrimage. You might sustain a few bumps and bruises, but you will not perish.

As you take this pilgrimage, remember that God is watching over you. He will not let your foot slip because He doesn't want you to fail. He wants to keep and protect you. You are important to Him, and He wants you to experience more than you currently are in Meshek, to experience the fullness of life. He wants you to experience Shalom.

Now, that's great news! Once you accept that God is your keeper, you'll carry that comfort with you the rest of your life. Consider this: God is there watching while you sleep (Verse 4). At 1:00 or 2:00 in the morning when you wake up panicked about your problems, you'll know that He has stationed His guard at your bedside. His presence is there. You can go back to sleep and let Him do His work.

A helpful way to focus on His presence with you is to speak His names and titles in your mind. I've found good results by using the alphabet to direct me. For example, I might say, "God, you are the Alpha, you're the Almighty, the Beginning, and the Bread of life. You are the Creator, the Christ, the Counselor, and Comforter," and so on through the alphabet. There are times when I wake up several hours later and realize I only got through the letter *G*. God is there as your keeper in the night hours. Acknowledge His presence at those times.

When you get up in the morning and go about your daily routine, you'll know that God is there at your right hand like a bodyguard. You'll acknowledge His presence as you open your eyes from sleep and read a portion of His Word early before starting the activities of your day. You'll talk to Him about the Bible passage you read, even if it's only a few verses. It will become so natural, because He's always there. You can't ignore someone who is constantly with you.

At work, God will be your keeper. He will keep you from getting scorched by your work even when things get heated through frustrations and difficulties. He is there to protect and guide you through problems. He already knows what you're going to face and is not surprised by the interruptions or crises that hit. He knew they were coming and He's ready.

If you anticipate an exceptionally difficult day ahead, be encouraged by these words from the Lord. God spoke them to the people of Israel as recorded in Deuteronomy 20:1-4:

> *When you go to war against your enemies and see horses and*
> *chariots and an army greater than yours, do not be afraid of them,*
> *because the Lord your God, who brought you up out of Egypt, will*

be with you. When you are about to go into battle, the priest shall
come forward and address the army. He shall say: "Hear, Israel:
Today you are going into battle against your enemies. Do not be
fainthearted or afraid; do not panic or be terrified by them. For the
Lord your God is the one who goes with you to fight for you against
your enemies to give you victory."

When a crisis hits, stop and acknowledge God's presence and lean on Him for help. He's not wringing His hands, saying, "Give me a minute. I'll think of something to help you." He already knows how to get you through the moment. In the evening when you come home, He comes home with you, not to rest from a busy day of watching over you, but to continue "keeping" you. As you face your family and the things that might be required of you there, stop and acknowledge His presence perhaps by praying with your family. At any moment of the day or night, you can turn to Him, take a deep breath, and say, "Okay, God. I'm ready. Let's go."

God is your keeper and He never takes a break. He doesn't have to. He's God, and He doesn't want a break because He's committed to "keeping" you. He has some changes to make in you, and you're going to like them if you remain steadfast in your search for Shalom.

But that's not all. The psalm goes on to say, "The Lord will watch over your coming and going both now and forevermore." That's an amazing statement. Don't miss the implications. As you learn to look to God constantly, He will watch over your coming and going both now and forevermore. He's in the "keeping" business in your life. It's a permanent commitment.

What you gain on this pilgrimage will get you through anything in life, not just what you're dealing with now but in all your future problems as well. You will be a new man who will not only be changed but will bring change to your world—change that will carry into eternity. You will experience the fullness of life that God intended for you, and your Shalom will bless others along the way.

So, to whom will you look on this pilgrimage? To whom will you look for help today, or when you return to Meshek? You have a choice. You can look to things of this earth or to the Maker of heaven and earth. Proverbs 3:5-6 reminds us to "Trust in the LORD with all your heart and lean not on your own understanding; in all your ways acknowledge him, and he will make your paths straight." Make it a daily practice to stop and acknowledge God as your keeper.

Discussion:

1. What about this pilgrimage, or the changes it might bring, makes you uneasy?
2. What about this pilgrimage excites you?
3. How does the phrase "Maker of heaven and earth" help you?
4. How can you start noting the presence of God throughout the night and day?
5. What tangible item could you place on your desk or keep in your pocket to remind you of God's continuous presence with and for you?

Chapter 3

Living in Spiritual Community

— PSALM 122 —

1 I rejoiced with those who said to me, "Let us go to the house of the Lord."

2 Our feet are standing in your gates, Jerusalem.

3 Jerusalem is built like a city that is closely compacted together.

4 That is where the tribes go up—the tribes of the Lord— to praise the name of the Lord according to the statute given to Israel.

5 There stand the thrones for judgment, the thrones of the house of David.

6 Pray for the peace of Jerusalem: "May those who love you be secure.

7 May there be peace within your walls and security within your citadels."

8 For the sake of my family and friends, I will say, "Peace be within you."

9 For the sake of the house of the Lord our God, I will seek
your prosperity.

W e've embarked on our pilgrimage, and hopefully it feels good to get away from Meshek, but we haven't yet talked much about where we're going. Psalm 122 introduces our destination—the house of the Lord in Jerusalem. It's the dwelling place of God's presence. Men in Old Testament times eagerly desired to take the pilgrimage to Jerusalem, and they sang these same psalms we're using on our pilgrimage. Their destination was the house of God, Zion, the place where they discovered Shalom.

You've probably lost certain things in life by living too long in Meshek, but you will discover that some of them weren't worth hanging onto. Paul wrote in Philippians 3:7-11:

> *But what things were gain to me, those I counted loss for Christ.*
> *Yea doubtless, and I count all things but loss for the excellency of the*
> *knowledge of Christ Jesus my Lord: for whom I have suffered the loss*
> *of all things, and do count them but dung, that I may win Christ,*
> *and be found in him, not having mine own righteousness, which*
> *is of the law, but that which is through the faith of Christ, the*
> *righteousness which is of God by faith: That I may know him, and*
> *the power of his resurrection, and the fellowship of his sufferings,*
> *being made conformable unto his death; If by any means I might*
> *attain unto the resurrection of the dead.*

On this pilgrimage, you will leave many things behind and gain many new things of much greater value. This psalm gives you a look at what you'll find at the end of our pilgrimage. Imagine yourself there. You've made the pilgrimage. You've found Shalom. What does it look like? This psalm provides a few details about our destination. They're described in the characteristics of the City of Zion. But before we look at those characteristics, we need to grasp the significance of Psalm 122's first line. It says, "I rejoiced with those who said to me, 'Let us go to the house of the Lord.'"

The key word is "us." Let "us" go to the house of the Lord. Our destination, the place where we find Shalom, is a place of spiritual community. It's a place where like-minded brothers live together and meet with God. You can't meet with God and not be changed. That is especially true in the context of community, where iron sharpens iron. Look how much people of the early church were changed as they met, worked, worshipped, and served in spiritual community. With that in mind, let's check out this city. What are some characteristics of the place in which we find Shalom?

1. The first characteristic is harmony. Our destination is a city "closely compacted together" or bound firmly together (See verse 3).

Most men balk at the idea of closeness. We want our space. Give me the wide-open spaces! To be in a place where we're closely compacted together might not sound inviting. But we have to understand the era in which this psalm was written. A walled city was a place of safety and strength. Those who lived outside the city, with plenty of open space, were vulnerable to the attacks of various enemies. A loner is an easy target. Likewise, a man who avoids the fellowship of other men is an easier target for the enemy of his soul.

A group of men, closely knit together, is hard to defeat. When a man stands alone, he is more vulnerable than when he's part of a like-minded group. Within the group in God's house, there is Shalom: well-being, tranquility, prosperity, and security. Men need union together with other men in like-mindedness, harmony, and fellowship, no longer separate or scattered.

Think of the offensive line on a football team. How closely knit are those men? They stand together to keep the opposition from getting to their quarterback. If they were too spread out, the enemy would penetrate every time and they would never score a touchdown. Each man on that team is part of the whole team. He does what he is assigned to do but in conjunction with the other team members. So it must be with the people of God.

A man who lives life alone becomes a man no one wants to be around. Such a man might have a family, maintain a job, and find himself around other people, but simply being around other people is not the same as *being* with them. A man who is with people shares his thoughts, feelings, frustrations, and goals. Most men find it hard to do this with women, especially their wives. Sometimes we're reticent to share because of fear. We're afraid to show our weaknesses. We fear that our weaknesses will negatively affect our relationships.

When men get together and share these kinds of issues among themselves, they experience harmony. That experience of harmony will carry over into all other areas of life. Back in Meshek, you might live around others with problems similar to yours, but there is no harmony, just coexistence and complaining.

The place where we're going is a place of true fellowship. We go there together and learn the value and enjoyment of pursuing the same goal. This is a critical lesson for those seeking Shalom. Commit now to fellowship with other godly men and begin to experience the harmony of Shalom.

2. The second characteristic is praise. The city is a place where we bring praise to God's name.

Some men have a hard time praising the Lord. If praise doesn't come naturally, you need to practice so that it flows from your mouth and heart. When you return to Meshek at the end of this pilgrimage, praise must be a natural part of your life. A good way to teach your heart and mouth to praise the Lord is by speaking select psalms to Him. For example, Psalm 91 begins with: "Whoever dwells in the shelter of the Most High will rest in the shadow of the Almighty. I will say of the Lord, 'He is my refuge and my fortress, my God, in whom I trust.'"

Using that verse, you might say aloud something like this: "Lord, you are my refuge and my fortress. You're my God and I fully trust in you." You might add certain specifics such as, "Since you are the Most High, I will rest in your presence. You are my refuge and fortress, therefore I trust you with the situation at work and/or home. I trust you with the health issue I'm facing and/or with the neighbor who is causing problems."

Continue through the psalm speaking God's thoughts back to Him with your circumstances in mind. As you practice praising God this way, you'll develop a heart for praise that will become an example for others back in Meshek. Right now, prayer and praise with others might be difficult for you, but as you practice it, especially aloud, it will become easier and be a great blessing back in Meshek.

3. The third characteristic of the city is justice. The city contains thrones of judgment where justice is found.

Everyone wants to be heard, and sometimes that's all we need. We long for someone who will listen to our complaint. We might not even win our case, but at least we've had the opportunity to present it without interruption. The destination of this pilgrimage is a place where complaints are heard and justice is carried out. God's house is where He sits on the throne, listening to your complaints so that He can mete out justice. The man who finds Shalom is a man who will listen to others and seek God's counsel. If he has treated others with injustice, he will not hesitate to make things right.

One way men often deal with injustice is to attack it. Back in Meshek, you may have created more problems than solutions by doing so. Seeking justice, God's way, works better than seeking it our way. We as men generally spend little time listening to others' complaints and more time jumping to conclusions. We want to attack the problem and conquer it now so we can get on with life. Remember, though, that God is very patient. That's His way of dealing with problems. Even when we were still in sin and without knowledge of God's forgiveness, He was patient with us, as Romans 2:4 says.

> *Don't you realize how patient He is with you, or don't you care? Can't you see that He has been waiting all this time without punishing you to give you time to turn from your sin? His kindness is meant to lead you to repentance.*

Another way we men often deal with injustice is to ignore it, but this only leads to frustration on the behalf of others. Don't let injustice go on. In patience and love, seek God's help and do something about it. We must learn to exercise justice, but with a listening ear and great patience. This will come as we spend time with God and learn from Him.

The intended result of this pilgrimage is that you will have gained the three characteristics of the city described in Psalm 122—harmony, praise, and justice—and that you will exhibit them in your life. These characteristics belong to the man who has experienced Shalom. Meditate on this psalm. Ask God to show you where you need to change and ask for His help.

Discussion:

1. Which of this psalm's three characteristics is most important to you?

2. Which of the three characteristics is hardest for you?
3. Pray for each man in your group to acquire these characteristics.
4. Use a psalm such as Psalm 93 to praise the Lord in your group. Have each man take one of the verses and speak it aloud to God.
5. Verse 8 says, "For the sake of my family and friends, I will say, 'Peace be with you.'" To learn the discipline of traveling together as a group of men, begin the habit of praying for the development of these characteristics in your fellow travelers. Also, consider greeting each other with: "Peace be with you and your family."

Chapter 4

Fight Contempt by Serving

— PSALM 123 —

1 I lift up my eyes to you, to you who sit enthroned in heaven.

2 As the eyes of slaves look to the hand of their master, as the eyes of a female slave look to the hand of her mistress, so our eyes look to the Lord our God, till he shows us his mercy.

3 Have mercy on us, Lord, have mercy on us, for we have endured no end of contempt.

4 We have endured no end of ridicule from the arrogant, of contempt from the proud.

The writer of Psalm 120 spoke of lies and deceit back in Meshek. He'd had enough and needed to get away. Here, in Psalm 123, the pilgrim mentions having to deal with ridicule from arrogant people and contempt from the proud. You might be experiencing some of these same frustrations in your Meshek. Certainly, we all as followers of Jesus, feel the contempt and ridicule of an anti-Christian world. American society is changing before our eyes with values that run counter to a Judeo-Christian culture. The culture is attacking Christians.

However, contemptuous attacks are sometimes brought on by people closest to us, people in our neighborhood, workplace, family, or even our church. Whatever the source, ridicule and contempt wear on a man and can only be tolerated for so long. They play on his self-image and often result in retaliation, which harms both him and those around him.

The word "contempt" is described in *The Treasury of David* (by Charles Spurgeon) as an acid which eats into the soul. Whether it's the disrespect of others or the circumstances of life that wear on us, the pain is real and deep. Men seem to be the target of much contempt these days. Television and movies depict men in general as incompetent idiots. Some men are treated as such by their wives or children. Other men experience disrespect or a better-than-thou attitude from coworkers, neighbors, and even people at church. Some people look down on a man because they have a better job, more money, or a bigger house.

If this is your experience, what should be your response? In Chapter 3, we were reminded that God is the righteous, sovereign judge. His judgments are complete and final. He will eventually make all things right. Such sin against you will be punished, or the perpetrator will change his or her ways through the forgiveness of the cross. Either way, the sin will be dealt with.

In this chapter, the pilgrim's cry is, "But what about now?" We know that God, the Righteous Judge, will eventually make all things right, but what about right now? What do we do about the contempt we face today? Is there no mercy?

Until God does make all things right, what should we do? According to Psalm 123, we are to act as servants who look to their Master for mercy. This may seem contrary to what our hearts tell us to do. Our natural inclination is to strike back at people who treat us poorly, but vengeance is not ours to mete out. Vengeance belongs to God. That's

His job and rightfully so since He sits on the highest throne. He is the ultimate and final judge.

The New Testament also teaches that we are not to seek vengeance. Rather, we are to live as children of the light and expose darkness. Consider the following verses:

Dear friends, never avenge yourselves. Leave that to God, for he has said that he will repay those who deserve it. Don't take the law into your own hands. (**Romans 12:19**)

Walk as children of light (for the fruit of light is found in all that is good and right and true). (**Ephesians 5:8-9**)

Take no part in the unfruitful works of darkness, but instead expose them. (**Ephesians 5:11**)

There's that word, "expose." We're to expose the deeds of darkness, the contemptuous actions of others, by faithfully and humbly serving our Master. It's not by striking back, or even by using words that we silence our critics. It's by our actions.

We must learn to act as servants of the Lord, recognizing and following His leading. God is the Master. We are the servants. We see things from below. He sits enthroned in heaven and sees things from above. He directs, and we follow. This lesson is illustrated by the psalmist in verse 2 when he says, "As the eyes of slaves look to the hand of their master . . . so our eyes look to the Lord our God, till he shows us his mercy."

The setting for this simple lesson could easily be a dinner party in which the master has invited several guests. The role of the servant is to serve the guests. That's our role, too. We serve those whom God has placed in our lives, for they are the ones He invited. Follow the action with me. Notice that the servant is not the center of attention in this picture. He stands aside, perhaps in a corner where he can see the guests and his master, but he himself is not seen.

When there is a need at the table, the master says nothing. He simply motions with his hand. The signal indicates that a guest needs his drink refreshed or more food. The servant, having learned the signals of his master, immediately responds. Nothing needs to be said. The signals say it all. As a result, the guests are impressed with the kindness and graciousness of their host. Yet it was the responsiveness of the servant, who knows his master well, that made the party a success.

It's often our feeble attempts to make things happen for God that bring the contempt of others upon us. Jesus clearly taught that servanthood is the way to greatness. In Mark 10:43, we read his words: "But whoever would be great among you must be your servant." Jesus not only taught this, but lived it. Meditate for a moment on the words of Philippians 2:5-9:

> *In your relationships with one another, have the same mindset as Christ Jesus: Who, being in very nature God, did not consider equality with God something to be used to his own advantage; rather, he made himself nothing by taking the very nature of a servant, being made in human likeness. And being found in appearance as a man, he humbled himself by becoming obedient to death—even death on a cross! Therefore God exalted him to the highest place.*

If you look closely, you'll probably agree that the people who are ridiculed are those who attempt to make themselves the center of attention. Those who humbly serve are honored.

Do you remember the following account recorded in John 13:12-17?

When he [Jesus] had finished washing their feet, he put on his clothes and returned to his place. "Do you understand what I have done for you?" he asked them. "You call me 'Teacher' and 'Lord' and rightly so, for that is what I am. Now that I, your Lord and Teacher, have washed your feet, you also should wash one another's feet. I have set you an example that you should do as I have done for you. I tell you the truth, no servant is greater than his master, nor is a messenger greater than the one who sent him. Now that you know these things, you will be blessed if you do them.

You might be very familiar with this passage, but have you ever noticed the last sentence? God's blessing—His mercy—comes with humble servanthood. So what does a servant do? He follows his master's signals. As Psalm 123 says, he looks to the hand of his master. How does the servant know the master's signals? He learns them by spending much time with the master. He studies him. He listens to him. Then he's ready when the master needs him.

Couples who live together for many years learn one another's signals. No words are necessary, just a glance or a slight indication of the hand. So it should be with us and God. How, then, do we serve our Master? We serve Him by being ready, watching Him intently, and responding immediately when He beckons us. In order to be ready, we need to understand His signals. This kind of ready response to the Master not only brings honor to Him but great joy to us, the servant. It's part of the Shalom experience.

People who don't know Christ have no clue as to who God is and what He desires. They don't know and they don't care. They have no knowledge of Him, let alone His signals. But we can know Him and experience the great joy of serving the Master—the One enthroned in heaven. That brings Shalom.

So, part of your search for Shalom is learning God's signals. Spend much time with Him. The more time you spend with Him, the more you will understand His signals. Get to know His plans and purposes. This comes from a regular, prayerful reading of and meditation on His Word. Observe the signals He gives through His indwelling Holy Spirit and do what He says. The more you fill yourself with God's Word, the more easily you will sense His prompting.

You might be ready to say something, and God will strongly impress on you not to say it. Likewise, He might prompt you to say or do something that *is* appropriate. You might have the urge to pray aloud with your family but are not comfortable doing so for lack of experience. Do it anyway. Keep the prayer short and simple. This is the role of the Master's servant. Start practicing today. Recognizing and following God's leading will bring you closer to the goal of experiencing Shalom.

You might wonder what the end of the psalm has to do with what we've discussed so far in this chapter. The psalmist says, "Have mercy on us, Lord. Have mercy on us for we have endured no end of contempt. We have endured no end of ridicule from the arrogant, of contempt from the proud."

Consider this: Contempt and ridicule from arrogant people is part of what drove the pilgrim to leave Meshek and seek Shalom in the City of God. He's looking for mercy from God. "Deliver me from all this!" is his cry, and deliverance comes through the discipline of servanthood. As we learn to fulfill the role of a servant of the Lord, seeking to learn His signals, we take on more of His true character.

We must learn to become like our Master who came as a servant and did not demand His own way. He cared more about others' needs than His own, He humbled Himself, and took up the towel to wash the disciples' feet. Such a person has received mercy. He has been freed from his own selfishness and pride. He can now enjoy who he is and flourish even in the face of arrogance and contempt. Furthermore, this man just might notice that the contempt of others is disappearing. The arrogant may no longer have anything more to say. Here's how Jesus put it: "Let your light shine before others, so that they may see your good works and give glory to your Father who is in heaven" (Matthew 5:16).

Discussion:
1. How have you or are you experiencing the ridicule or contempt of others?
2. How does this chapter help you better handle the contempt and ridicule of others?
3. Explain how you have experienced God's "signals" in your life.
4. Talk about your current Bible reading habit and discuss how you could improve it so as to learn God's signals.

Chapter 5

Remember Former Deliverances

1 If the Lord had not been on our side—let Israel say—

2 if the Lord had not been on our side when people attacked us,

3 they would have swallowed us alive when their anger flared against us;

4 the flood would have engulfed us, the torrent would have swept over us,

5 the raging waters would have swept us away.

6 Praise be to the Lord, who has not let us be torn by their teeth.

7 We have escaped like a bird from the fowler's snare; the snare has been broken, and we have escaped.

8 Our help is in the name of the Lord, the Maker of heaven and earth.

Many of our frustrations in life come from people. It was people problems that caused the writer of Psalm 120 to essentially say, "I've got to get out of here!" He looks back at a time when people "attacked . . . when their anger flared up against us." What does it feel like when you're attacked by people? The psalmist compares his anguish to being swallowed alive or swept away in a raging flood. How do your people problems make you feel?

In this chapter, we'll look back at some of the problems we've faced, whether caused by other people or not, and remember how God delivered us. Take a moment to think about a past experience when you needed God's deliverance. Maybe you hurt so badly you cried out to Him for help. How painful was that experience? How did God deliver you from it and how did you feel after you were delivered? What did you learn from that experience about yourself, about other people, and about God?

The challenge in this chapter is to learn to turn pain into praise. Our natural response to painful experiences is to complain. However, praising the Lord lifts us above the difficulty whereas complaining takes us deeper into self-pity. Like the writer of Psalm 124, it helps to recall how we felt during former troubles then the way we felt when God delivered us and let that become praise. With this psalm, we'll take our cue from the writer and look back at former times in our lives when God delivered us, specifically remembering how He delivered us. It's an exercise in praise.

In Psalm 122, we looked at the destination of the pilgrimage. It's the House of the Lord. It is a place where men praise the name of the Lord. There, we saw that a man can learn to praise God by using the phrases and statements of Scripture. Here, we learn to praise God by telling others of His goodness. Instead of complaining about our problems, we'll lift up praise to the Lord in the presence of others by telling our story. Such praise is both pleasing to the Lord and instructive to others.

When telling your story, don't minimize the pain you felt or even how you got mad at God. However, the focus of your praise should be on how God delivered or is delivering you.

Praise can be a bit awkward. That's because we're not used to it. The more we practice praise the more natural it becomes. An easy way to praise is to simply tell your testimony of deliverance. Psalm 73 is an example of a man turning pain into praise. There, Asaph tells how troubled he was with people who spoke with malice and arrogance and who threatened oppression against him. He writes:

They scoff, and speak with malice; with arrogance they threaten oppression. (**Verse 8**)

When I tried to understand all this, it troubled me deeply. (**Verse 16**)

He responds by feeling sorry for himself.

Surely in vain I have kept my heart pure and have washed my hands in innocence. All day long I have been afflicted, and every morning brings new punishments. (**Verses 13-14**)

Later in the psalm, he admits how foolish he was to react this way and turns his bitterness into praise, realizing that "God is the strength of my heart and my portion forever" (Verse 26). He ends the psalm with this line: "I will tell of all your deeds" (Verse 28). That's the challenge for you on this step of our pilgrimage.

Some men have a past experience of God's deliverance from a difficult time or event in life. Some men may have lived such an experience but have not yet seen deliverance. Other men may be in the process of receiving God's deliverance. As you share your story, others will be instructed and encouraged. Maybe you have no story of God's deliverance, but you are in need of deliverance from something you're currently going through. Share that with other men and express your desire to be delivered. By expressing a deep desire for God's deliverance, acknowledging that only He can deliver you, you are praising Him.

Sometimes, like the writer of this psalm, we find ourselves in such difficult and dangerous circumstances that there is no way out except by the hand of our merciful God. The repetition of the phrase "if the Lord had not been on our side" emphasizes the severity of the situation. But praise doesn't have to be based on one terrible incident that occurred in our lives. It can simply be looking back at a difficult time in life that God brought you through safely.

Sharing your story with your brothers will remind you that you are weak but God is strong. It helps you remember that you don't succeed by your strength but by God's strength. In remembering the good times, we may focus on our own abilities, but in remembering the bad times, we focus on God and His goodness.

Look again at the last line of Psalm 124. "Our help is in the name of the Lord, the Maker of heaven and earth." We sometimes hear people talk about a person's good name. They're really talking about that person's character. The "name" of the Lord represents His character. So, in praising God for His deliverance, we talk about His character. We've seen so far on this pilgrimage that God is the Maker of heaven and earth, he's our Keeper, our refuge and fortress, and he's merciful. These are just a few of His awesome attributes that deserve our praise.

Psalm 77 is another example of a man remembering the deliverance of the Lord. The psalmist begins with expressions of anguish, saying: "I cried out to God for help; I cried out to God to hear me." But by verse 10, he turns his pain into praise by remembering what God has done for him: "Then I thought, "to this I will appeal; the years when the Most High stretched out his right hand. I will remember the deeds of the

Lord; yes, I will remember your miracles long ago. I will consider all your works and meditate on all your mighty deeds."

Another example of turning pain into praise and giving honor to His name is found in 2 Samuel 22. David sang this song to the Lord when the Lord delivered him from his enemies and the hand of Saul. In it, he talks about his feelings when pursued. "The waves of death swirled about me; the torrents of destruction overwhelmed me" (Verses 5-6). The psalm is filled with praises to the name of God: "my rock, my shield, my stronghold." He also describes how the Lord delivered him when he says: "He brought me out into a spacious place" (Verse 20).

Take some time to put together your story of God's deliverance and share it with a brother or with your group. Practice this pattern of turning pain into praise. It will be a powerful resource for maintaining Shalom when you're back in Meshek.

Discussion:

1. Share a short story of God's provision or intervention in your life. It could be your salvation story or something else. It doesn't have to be dramatic.

2. What characteristic of God's nature is revealed through your story?

3. Spend a few minutes in prayer simply telling God how much you appreciate those aspects of His character.

Chapter 6

Don't Get All Shook Up

— PSALM 125 —

1 Those that trust in the Lord are like Mount Zion, which cannot be shaken but endures forever.

2 As the mountains surround Jerusalem, so the Lord surrounds his people both now and forevermore.

3 The scepter of the wicked will not remain over the land allotted to the righteous, for then the righteous might use their hands to do evil.

4 Lord, do good to those who are good, to those who are upright in heart.

5 But those who turn to crooked ways the Lord will banish with the evildoers. Peace be on Israel.

How did our world and our nation get into such a mess and how did it happen so quickly? Every radio or television news cast starts with the account of another murder, hit and run accident, mass shooting, or terrorist attack. It seems that this is all we talk about these days, and we ask how it all happened so quickly. It's unsettling. It can shake us to the very core.

In addition to such violence, we see a rapid erosion of morality. How can these things be happening? They seem unstoppable. For some of us, we see this kind of chaos occurring in our families, our workplaces, and even in our churches. "Where is God? Why isn't He doing something about this?" we ask, but Jesus warned us of these things long ago when He spoke about the end times.

As he sat on the Mount of Olives, the disciples came to him privately, saying, "Tell us, when will these things be, and what will be the sign of your coming and of the end of the age?" And Jesus answered them, "See that no one leads you astray. For many will come in my name, saying, 'I am the Christ,' and they will lead many astray. And you will hear of wars and rumors of wars. See that you are not alarmed, for this must take place, but the end is not yet. For nation will rise against nation, and kingdom against kingdom, and there will be famines and earthquakes in various places. All these are but the beginning of the birth pains. Then they will deliver you up to tribulation and put you to death, and you will be hated by all nations for my name's sake. And then many will fall away and betray one another and hate one another. And many false prophets will arise and lead many astray. And because lawlessness will be increased, the love of many will grow cold."
Matthew 24:3-12

The Apostle Paul writes about the last days in 2 Timothy 3:1-5, saying:

But understand this that in the last days there will come times of difficulty. For people will be lovers of self, lovers of money, proud, arrogant, abusive, disobedient to their parents, ungrateful, unholy, heartless, unappeasable, slanderous, without self-control, brutal, not loving good, treacherous, reckless, swollen with conceit, lovers of pleasure rather than lovers of God, having the appearance of godliness, but denying its power.

It really should be no surprise to us. We were told that this would happen before the return of our Lord. Is He coming back soon? We don't know how soon but we know that we are to live as though it could be very soon. So here's the lesson of Psalm 125: don't be shaken by all this.

We certainly can and should be concerned, but we must not be shaken. The person who is shaken is the one who falls away. That's the meaning of the word "shaken" in this psalm. The Hebrew word is *Mot* meaning to waiver, slip, or fall. In case we think that this couldn't happen to us, we should be reminded of the following warnings from Scripture:

See to it, brothers and sisters, that none of you has a sinful, unbelieving heart that turns away from the living God. But encourage one another daily, as long as it is called "Today," so that none of you may be hardened by sin's deceitfulness. **(Hebrews 3:12-13)**

Then you will be handed over to be persecuted and put to death, and you will be hated by all nations because of me. At that time many will turn away from the faith. **(Matthew 24:9-10)**

What, then, can keep us from being shaken? According to this psalm, it's a trust in the Lord. Verse 1 says, "Those who trust in the Lord are like Mount Zion, which cannot be shaken but endures forever." That word, "endure," means to sit down or to dwell. It refers to something solid and permanent. It's not going anywhere. It exudes confidence, but confidence in what? Today, many are putting confidence in themselves, but for we who seek Shalom it must be confidence in something or someone more solid than us. That something or someone is the Lord.

At this point, you might be saying, "I know all this." Okay, then let's get very practical and be honest with ourselves. If we know it but we're still shaken by the evil in the world, something is wrong. What is it?

Let's first see what it looks like to be shaken. Then we'll look at the solution given in the psalm. Signs of being shaken include fear, impatience, anger, and increasing periods of frustration or depression. Have you ever noticed that you're more stirred up after watching the news, and, by becoming so shaken, you bring frustration and fear to those around you? This is the opposite of Shalom.

Our goal is to find Shalom and help others find it too. Instability in our lives will only breed more instability. It steals peace from our lives. We're supposed to bring Shalom wherever we interact with others. But if we are unstable when faced with evil, we will bring about instability for all those around us. However, if we're stable, we'll manifest Shalom and bring stability to our whole environment. Ultimately, our goal is not only to experience Shalom, but also to bring it to the lives of those around us.

There are many things besides evil that tend to shake us, including job insecurity, financial problems, health issues, and broken relationships. These add to our lack of stability and negatively affect those in our world. How can we learn to experience Shalom in all circumstances?

Let's look at the solution provided in Psalm 125. The writer says that trusting in the Lord is the solution. "Trust" is the key. In what are we to trust? Let it not be ourselves or in better circumstances. It must be a trust in the Lord who is like the mountains surrounding Jerusalem. We become solid and unshaken when we attach ourselves to a greater power that is more solid than us, not unlike an elderly man who holds onto his walker. It's the walker which gives him stability. Likewise, when we cling to God, it is He who gives us stability. After all, He is the Maker of heaven and earth. This is a huge but difficult lesson to learn for many men.

We're all familiar with Philippians 4:6-7, which says, "Be anxious for nothing, but in everything by prayer and supplication with thanksgiving let your requests be made known to God. And the peace of God, which surpasses all comprehension, shall guard your hearts and your minds in Christ Jesus." The key to that passage is found in Psalm 125. In order to be anxious for nothing, we need to cling to the Lord. Once again, let's get very practical and honest.

If you find that you're easily shaken, you need to ask why. The answer is not found in others or in your circumstances. The answer is within you—in your belief system. It may be that your understanding of God is incorrect.

Two things you need to know about God are found in this psalm, the first being that the Lord surrounds His people both now and forevermore. Do you believe that? You should. He's got your present and future (your forever) in His care. Regarding this psalm in his book, *Expositions of the Holy Scripture:* Psalms, Alexander MacLaren writes, "The simple act of trust in God brings inward stability." The Hebrew word for trust here means to hang onto. In other words, to trust God is to fasten ourselves to Him. Therefore, as MacLaren says, "There is one way to make them stable, and only one; and that is that they shall be fastened, as it were, to that which is stable, and so be steadfast because they hold by what is steadfast." When we fasten ourselves to God—the stable one—we become like Him: stable.

So, if you were to die in an act of terrorism today, what would happen to you? If you belong to God through your faith in Jesus Christ, you would be with Him in heaven because you're fastened to Him. Sure, that's good for me, you say, but what about my loved ones who are left behind? That's an honest question, but we must be able to comprehend the fact that God is with them too. God is big enough and loving enough to take care of them even in their grief. Their ultimate comfort is not in your presence but in God's presence.

The second aspect about God found in this psalm is this: "The scepter of the wicked will not remain over the land allotted to the righteous, for then the righteous might use their hands to do evil" (Verse 3). Do you believe that?

God promises to eradicate evil in the end, not now. For now, He has promised Shalom in the midst of evil. Are you willing to forgo the demise of evil in your lifetime in order to become strong in the battle against evil for the sake of others? In Acts 4, the Apostles were imprisoned and prayed not for release or protection but for boldness to serve God more. Shalom does not mean that everything is going our way but that we know God knows what He is doing and is in control of all things. That gives us the ability to live life to the full.

Those who fail to grasp this truth are in danger of becoming so discouraged that they may fall into evil. Where there is no hope, people often turn to destructive ways that hurt themselves and others. Our children and grandchildren are negatively affected by this kind of reaction to discouragement on our part. Yet, the testimony of our lives, as men who have experienced Shalom, can be a strong deterrent to such disaster.

A man experiencing Shalom has learned to say, "I trust you, Lord." From that trust, he draws peace and brings peace to a crazy world. Even if everyone else remains shaken, he remains unshaken. He is the stability for those around him, and this comes not from himself but from God. It doesn't happen once. God provides this strength daily. It's with this perspective that Christian martyrs of past and present have remained unshaken. The testimony of their lives gives us strength and the testimony of our lives will give strength to others.

Jesus said He did not come to eliminate evil from the world, but so that the kingdom of God can grow amid the evil in the world until the time when all evil is destroyed by Him. We cannot eliminate all evil in the world, but we can and should do our best to minimize the suffering it causes and to bring Shalom to those who will receive it. Although we cannot eliminate all evil and suffering, people who develop great faith in God often find an inner peace that simply overshadows the evils of the world and the suffering they endure.

Becoming unshakable is part of the process of finding Shalom. Many things in your life can shake or unnerve you. The world in which you live—the world at large as well as your Meshek—is overrun with evil and evil people. That is not going to change until God, through Jesus Christ, puts an end to it and brings His peace. We need to understand God's purposes and timetable and accept them.

When you're back in Meshek, you will need to surround people as the mountains surround Jerusalem and teach them, by your example, to trust in the Lord and not be shaken. Your testimony, like that of the martyrs, will lead them to Him and embolden them. That doesn't mean that you hide your fears and concerns. Be real. Be honest, but let others see the strength that comes from trust in the Lord.

This psalm is a reminder that the rule of unrighteousness (the scepter of the wicked) will not last forever. It will come to an end. God will do this. That's His job. For now, His people, who learn to trust the Lord, will bring peace in the midst of the storm. That's our job.

The world's situation today and the situation in your Meshek can cause fear and doubt about ever being able to bring peace to your world. When looking at the people or circumstances in your life, you might also wonder if the situation is hopeless. Everything seems unstable and that's exactly what our enemy, the devil, wants to create—instability, uncertainty, fear, and chaos. Our prayers seem to get no answers so we get discouraged. The answer is in this psalm. God is allowing evil to run its full course. God may not change the outward circumstances, but He will change our hearts to experience strength and peace.

Shalom is the only antidote to the evil in our world and that's why God is making you a man capable of experiencing and sharing Shalom. When you become stable through your trust in the Lord, you will bring stability to your chaotic world. In the words of this psalm, you are becoming like Mount Zion, which cannot be shaken but endures forever. The key word is "trust." Learn to say this little phrase every day, "Lord, I trust you." You become that man of peace, that stability in a chaotic world, by learning to trust in the Lord. Notice that you will be this way forever. You'll take this characteristic to heaven with you.

Discussion:

1. What causes you or people in your life to be shaken?
2. What's the difference between being concerned and being shaken?
3. In what ways have you brought instability into your world by being shaken?
4. Pray for each other to become men of stability.
5. Read Daniel 7:9-14.
6. Meditate on these verses: Psalm 4:8, Psalm 119:165, John 14:27, 2 Corinthians 4:16-17.

Chapter 7

Sacrifice May Be Required

— PSALM 126 —

1 When the Lord restored the fortunes of Zion, we were like those who dreamed.

2 Our mouths were filled with laughter, our tongues with songs of joy. Then it was said among the nations, "The Lord has done great things for them."

3 The Lord has done great things for us, and we are filled with joy.

4 Restore our fortunes, Lord, like streams in the Negev.

5 Those who sow with tears will reap with songs of joy.

6 Those who go out weeping, carrying seed to sow, will return with songs of joy, carrying sheaves with them.

"Some assembly required." That comment on the box can give a guy the shivers, especially if he is not mechanically inclined. Knowing that, products that need assembly prominently display the beautiful assembled product, not the parts, on the front of the package. The message about assembly being required is placed somewhere else on the package so as not to discourage the buyer from the get-go.

Seeing the finished product provides the motivation to purchase the product, open the box, and get started with the assembly process. It's the same with this pilgrimage. If we only see the process of seeking Shalom, we might become discouraged and give up along the way. It's not an easy journey but it is definitely rewarding.

In Chapter 6, we saw the necessity of being attached to God if we are ever going to experience Shalom. What is it like to be attached to God? Think about it. God is not sitting in a rocking chair sipping lemonade. He is the Warrior King who is bringing all things to a conclusion and will ultimately put an end to evil. Attaching yourself to Him will bring stability to your life, but the process is a wild ride. It's going to take some sacrifice on your part.

Sacrifice is the subject of this chapter. Sacrifice is part of the process of change that we're going through in search of Shalom. In Chapter 1, you were asked to talk about what you lost by living in Meshek. At the time, you may not have been able to identify anything in particular. Perhaps now you can. We pointed out that Shalom incorporates the ideas of favor, prosperity, safety, wellbeing, tranquility, harmony within and without, restored relationships, and vigor and vitality in all dimensions of life.

What have you lost by living too long in Meshek? Psalm 126 pictures a restoration of things lost. Imagine what it would be like to get them back or better yet, to receive from God that which is even better than that which was lost. Think of Job. His loss was huge but the Lord restored his fortunes, blessing him in his latter days more than in the beginning (Job 42:10-16).

This process of restoration requires some assembly. Psalm 126 makes that clear when it says, "Those who sow with tears" and "those who go out weeping, carrying seed to sow" will be the ones who return with joy carrying sheaves with them. The tears and weeping represent sacrifice. Generally, we don't like to sacrifice. We like our comforts. A little challenge now and again is fine, but a steady diet of sacrifice is generally avoided.

However, no good thing comes to us without some sacrifice. There is a cost to finding Shalom, but if we just look at the cost, we might decide it's not worth the effort. Just like the people of Israel in the desert, we might decide to go back to "Egypt," or in our case, Meshek, and forget about the pilgrimage. Because of this, the psalm starts with a look at the finished product to give us the needed motivation.

For the pilgrim in Psalm 126, the finished product is his life restored. That which he lost, or never had in Meshek, is now restored and there is great joy. Listen to the passion in the words of the psalmist: "When the Lord restored the fortunes of Zion, we were like those who dreamed. Our mouths were filled with laughter, our tongues with songs of joy. Then it was said among the nations, "The Lord has done great things for them."

Wouldn't it be great to laugh again—to smile at your life? We're told that great things are coming, things that will fill us with joy and laughter. Then what about this sacrifice? It's reported in verses five and six that those who go out weeping, carrying seed to sow, will return with songs of joy, carrying sheaves with them. If the Lord is to restore that which we have lost, it's going to take some tears and some planting of seeds on our part. It's the sowing and reaping process. What are you willing to give up in order to get back what you lost in Meshek? Consider the words of Jesus recorded in John 12:23-26:

And Jesus answered them, "The hour has come for the Son of Man to be glorified. Truly, truly, I say to you, unless a grain of wheat falls into the earth and dies, it remains alone; but if it dies, it bears much fruit. Whoever loves his life loses it, and whoever hates his life in this world will keep it for eternal life. If anyone serves me, he must follow me; and where I am, there will my servant be also. If anyone serves me, the Father will honor him."

Life comes after death. It's the principle of dying to self and sin. That's what brings the abundant life that Jesus spoke of in John 10:10. "The thief comes only to steal and kill and destroy. I came that they may have life and have it abundantly."

The Apostle Paul knew that this was not a one-time event but a way of life, as evidenced in the following verses:

I face death every day. (**1 Corinthians 15:31**)

We always carry around in our body the death of Jesus, so that the life of Jesus may also be revealed in our body. (**2 Corinthians 4:10**)

What might God be asking you to die to in order to get those aspects of Shalom that you lost or never had in Meshek?
   • Wanting to be right all the time
   • Being first
   • My comforts
   • My goals
   • My way
   • My time
   • My pride
   • My little sins

Is it worth giving up these things in order to get Shalom, which is far better?

It's said that Jesus, "who for the joy that was set before him endured the cross, despising the shame, and is seated at the right hand of the throne of God" (Hebrews 12:2). Think of what He gave up and what He gained (Philippians 2).

If we don't get back all of our losses in this life, we certainly will gain them and more in the next. For our Lord and for us, the promise is pictured in Revelation 5:9-10:

> *And they sang a new song, saying: "You are worthy to take the scroll and to open its seals, because you were slain, and with your blood you purchased for God persons from every tribe and language and people and nation. You have made them to be a kingdom and priests to serve our God, and they will reign on the earth."*

However, we don't have to wait for the next life to experience Shalom. The promise of Jesus is "Peace I leave with you; my peace I give you. I do not give to you as the world gives. Do not let your hearts be troubled and do not be afraid" (John 14:27).

Although the Shalom we receive through this pilgrimage will require sacrifice, it will bring unbridled joy and we will testify with the pilgrim of this psalm:

> *When the Lord restored the fortunes of Zion, we were like those who dreamed. Our mouths were filled with laughter, our tongues with songs of joy. Then it was said among the nations, "The Lord has done great things for them." The Lord has done great things for us, and we are filled with joy.*

Discussion:

1. To what do you need to die in order to regain what you lost or never even had?
2. What sacrifice will you make to experience Shalom and bring it into your life?

Chapter 8

Let God Build Your House

— PSALM 127 —

1 Unless the Lord builds the house, the builders labor in vain. Unless the Lord watches over the city, the guards stand watch in vain.

2 In vain you rise early and stay up late, toiling for food to eat—for he grants sleep to those he loves.

3 Children are a heritage from the Lord, offspring a reward from him.

4 Like arrows in the hands of a warrior are children born in one's youth.

5 Blessed is the man whose quiver is full of them. They will not be put to shame when they contend with their opponents in court.

M en are builders. That's what we do. We build houses and cities. We build businesses and careers. We build churches and families. We build a life for ourselves and the ones we love. God has made us to be builders and every man wants success in his building endeavors.

49

According to Psalm 127, there is a right way and a wrong way to build. Building takes effort. But the efforts of a man can backfire if he goes about it the wrong way. Psalm 127 contains a key word. It's mentioned three times. The word is "vain." Notice the recurrence of that word.

Unless the Lord builds the house, the builders labor in vain.

Unless the Lord watches over the city, the guards stand watch in vain.

In vain you rise early and stay up late, toiling for food to eat.

That word "vain" is a strong word. To the English reader, it means empty, useless, or unprofitable. In the original Hebrew, the word is Shav and it literally means destructive, evil, or idolatrous. The difference is striking. In other words, our striving to make something good happen can actually bring harm to us and others in our world. Rather than accomplishing the desired result, our vain efforts actually become destructive and evil.

Many a man has lived to regret the way he chose to build. His efforts, rather than bringing good reward, have brought evil on his family. He may gain a house or a career but lose his more precious possessions. "Children are a heritage from the Lord, offspring a reward from him," says the psalm. Don't build in such a manner that you destroy them.

Psalm 127 is really all about relationships. It's about our children— our families, whether it's the nuclear family, the church family, or extended family. God puts people in our lives to develop and strengthen us. It's through these close relationships that we grow and are blessed. Blessed is the man whose quiver is full of them.

Unsurprisingly, this chapter's lesson is to let God build your relationships. We men tend to have a hard time with relationships. The effort we put into relationship building is similar to the way we shop—which is infrequent and fast. When we shop, we're on a mission. Get in, get it, and get out. That doesn't work with relationship building.

When there are problems in relationships, we might think that the harder and faster we "build," the better the relationships will turn out. However, sometimes we try so hard to get it done that we drive people away. At the beginning of this pilgrimage, the man in Psalm 120 knew things weren't right in his hometown and he couldn't wait to get out or, at least, to change things. That's what we men do when we can't seem to control our situation.

When things aren't happening the way we planned and people aren't responding the way we think they should, we try to force change. But when that doesn't work, we stop trying and simply remove ourselves from the problem. Some men even leave for good. None of those options is the correct one. The correct solution is to depend on God and let Him bring about change. Psalm 127 warns that without God at the center of our efforts, all our striving becomes useless or even worse. We must depend on Him in all of our building endeavors.

Zechariah 4:6 says, "This is the word of the LORD to Zerubbabel: 'Not by might nor by power, but by my Spirit,' says the LORD Almighty." In its historical context, this verse speaks of the Jewish exiles from Babylon on their return to the Promised Land where they were terribly discouraged. They had been there sixteen years yet had not been able to finish the work of rebuilding the temple. After all their efforts, the temple was still unimpressive and unfinished, just like some of our relationships. Without the temple, the glory and prosperity of the people would not exist in their eyes.

This message of God through the prophet Zechariah was one of encouragement to men who were trying hard but failing to succeed with their plans. God was not criticizing their efforts. Their desire to build a beautiful tabernacle for Him was commendable. But He was reminding them that the work was His and that He would accomplish it. God knows how to build relationships. Remember, He is the one who "reconciled us to himself through Christ and gave us the ministry of reconciliation" (2 Corinthians 5:18).

We men often look with discouragement at the poor condition of our family, of the church, or of the workplace and we determine that we will bring about change through our efforts. We make a plan and, of course, we ask God to bless the plan we've made. Then we excitedly put all our efforts into it, trying to make it work. However, when it doesn't turn out well, we become discouraged. We get mad and either apply more force to make it happen or we get frustrated and abandon the cause. In either case, the end result is vain efforts. We find that we've caused more trouble than if we had never tried to fix the problem in the first place.

Given all this, it should be clear that God is the one who does the building and protecting of our relationships through us. This doesn't mean that we do nothing, expecting God to do all the work. It takes a cooperative effort in which God works His power, wisdom, and character through us to bring about His success. We like the part about His power and wisdom but what about His character?

Let's look for a moment at 2 Corinthians 5:15 where the Apostle Paul explains how reconciliation works: "And he [Christ] died for all, that those who live should no longer live for themselves but for him who died for them and was raised again." He's saying that as men, for whom Christ died, we have one goal in life and that is to live for Him. Our every effort is to be expended, not on ourselves, but on His plan. In Christ, we're different that other men. We have been changed, including our whole attitude.

Verse 16 goes on to explain that change by saying, "from now on we regard no one from a worldly point of view." We see them differently, from Christ's point of view. What was Christ's point of view? He came to serve, not to be served. When we begin to serve others—our wives, our children, our coworkers, our neighbors, or friends at church—our world begins to change. In Christ, as new creatures, we no longer live for ourselves but for Christ and we no longer look at others the way we used to look at them. We look at them, not to get from them, but to give to them. Then God does His work. That's the way God builds and protects your house.

When we are in Christ, God gives us His presence through the indwelling Holy Spirit. Through His Word and His promptings, He transforms us into men who can change the way things can be back in Meshek. It's all part of the process of finding Shalom.

Consider, prayerfully, the fruit that the Spirit of God wants to bring to your life as recorded in Galatians 5:22-23. The fruit of the Spirit are:

- Love
- Joy
- Peace
- Forbearance
- Kindness
- Goodness
- Faithfulness
- Gentleness
- Self-control

Ask God to build each of these qualities into your life so that He may build your house through you.

Discussion:
1. In what ways have you been trying to force results in your relationships?
2. How could you approach your relationships differently by applying the fruit of the Spirit?

3. Which "fruit" is missing from your life more than the others?
4. How would the presence of that "fruit" change the way people respond to you?
5. Meditate on and memorize Galatians 5:22-23.

Chapter 9

Walk God's Road

— PSALM 128 —

1 Blessed are all who fear the Lord, who walk in obedience to him.

2 You will eat the fruit of your labor; blessings and prosperity will be yours.

3 Your wife will be like a fruitful vine within your house; your children will be like olive shoots around your table.

4 Yes, this will be the blessing for the man who fears the Lord.

5 May the Lord bless you from Zion; may you see the prosperity of Jerusalem all the days of your life.

6 May you live to see your children's children—peace be on Israel.

Lest we forget why we're on this pilgrimage, we're in search of Shalom. Just like the man in Psalm 120, we want to get away from those things that cause strife and embrace life the way God intended it to be. Like him, we want our efforts to prosper and our relationships to be successful. Simply put, we're looking for God's blessing. Psalm 128 tells us up front that God's blessing is experienced by those who "fear the Lord, who walk in obedience to him."

To "fear" God and to "walk in obedience to him" are not two separate things. They're different ways of saying the same thing. To fear God means to respect Him for who He is. He's the Lord, our Master, the Maker of heaven and earth. To walk in obedience to Him literally means to walk "on His road." The Hebrew word used here for "walk" is *Darak*, which is used several times in Scripture for walking on a road. Therefore, in order to receive God's blessing, we must walk on God's road. That's where Shalom is found. You'll never find it by walking another road.

There seem to be many roads a person may take in this life, but according to the Bible, there are just two. One leads to destruction and the other to life everlasting. God's road is the way to life and that road begins and ends with Jesus. Jesus Himself said, "I am the way and the truth and the life. No one comes to the Father except through me." Proverbs 16:25 tells about the other road: "There is a way that appears to be right, but in the end it leads to death." Death represents separation, a separation from God and all that He intended for your life. God's road is the way of blessing. God's road is the way to Shalom. All other roads are simply ways that lead away from God and His blessing. They separate us from God.

In Chapter 8, we saw the necessity of letting the Lord build our relationships in order to receive His blessing. In this psalm, we see that God's blessings are always found on His road, because that's where He walks. In fact, the blessings come from His presence which is found on His road. Psalm 16:11 says, "You make known to me the path of life; you will fill me with joy in your presence, with eternal pleasures at your right hand." The search for Shalom, which includes good personal relationships, requires that you walk the path set out by God.

Although a man might acknowledge that the correct road is God's road, there are times when even the most devoted traveler veers off that road. Rather than continuing to seek God's way, a man sometimes chooses to take a side road. It may be that he is tired of the straight and narrow way and is attracted by the ways of the world around him, or he might feel that his efforts to maintain the course are not accomplishing what he desires.

Sometimes men veer off God's road because men who choose other roads seem to prosper more. The writer of Psalm 73 admitted that after seeing the apparently easy life of many non-believers, he became weary of being good. These are his words:

But as for me, my feet had almost slipped; I had nearly lost my foothold. For I envied the arrogant when I saw the prosperity of the wicked. They have no struggles; their bodies are healthy and strong. They are free from common human burdens; they are not plagued by human ills . . . All in vain have I kept my heart clean and washed my hands in innocence.
Psalm 73:2-5, 13

Let's admit it. There are times when we feel the same way and wonder what it would be like to take a side road just to experience something a little different. Fortunately for the psalmist, he stopped before making a tragic mistake. Instead of dwelling on the tantalizing possibilities of a diversion, he brought his feelings to God and spent time in His presence where he was brought to his senses with the reality that those who take a different road are "on slippery ground" that leads to destruction (Verses 18 and 19). He confessed his foolish thinking before it was too late and acknowledged the great benefits of staying on God's road. If you find yourself tempted by another path, stop and frankly talk to God about your feelings as the psalmist does here in verses 13-28:

Surely in vain have I kept my heart pure; in vain have I washed my hands in innocence. All day long I have been plagued; I have been punished every morning. If I had said, "I will speak thus," I would have betrayed your children. When I tried to understand all this, it was oppressive to me till I entered the sanctuary of God; then I understood their final destiny. Surely you place them on slippery ground; you cast them down to ruin. How suddenly are they destroyed, completely swept away by terrors! As a dream when one awakes, so when you arise, O Lord, you will despise them as fantasies. When my heart was grieved and my spirit embittered, I was senseless and ignorant; I was a brute beast before you. Yet I am always with you; you hold me by my right hand. You guide me with your counsel, and afterward you will take me into glory. Who have I in heaven but you? And earth has nothing I desire besides you. My flesh and my heart may fail, but God is the strength of my heart and my portion forever. Those who are far from you will perish; you destroy all who are unfaithful to you. But as for me, it is good to be near God. I have made the Sovereign LORD my refuge; I will tell of all your deeds.

Another helpful passage is Psalm 139:23-24. There, David invites God to search him and know his heart to see if there is any wickedness in him. The English Standard Version changes the word "wicked" to "grievous," which provides a more accurate understanding of what's being said. The Hebrew word is Otseb, which refers to an idol that leads to grief. Therefore, a wicked way is a grievous path that leads away from God. It's a different road, not God's road. It's a substitute for God, an idol that brings grief. It may not look grievous to the traveler on God's road. In fact, it might look very attractive, like the tree of the knowledge of good and evil looked to Eve. However, once taken, that path becomes an obvious bad choice.

I like to call the attractive side road a comfort path. It's something, like comfort food, that provides consolation in the moment, but eventually leads to grief. Men often seek these comfort paths in a time of frustration or stress. The comfort feels good at the start but is always short-lived. Like a sugar rush, it feels good for a moment then sends us crashing. Because these activities are sinful, they lead to grief. If a man is ever going to experience Shalom, he must learn to stay on God's road and avoid the sinful paths. It's a discipline that must be exercised every day, all day.

Some men under stress seek comfort in extra-marital affairs or pornography. Others soothe their discomfort by indulging in alcohol or drugs. Some men overwork just to avoid problems at home. However, a grievous path may not be inherently bad. It may be a hobby or an avocation. It may be television or books. However, to be classified as idolatrous it's always something that replaces God in our lives. It takes us off God's road.

David ends Psalm 139 with this statement, "Lead me in the way everlasting." In other words, put me back on your road. If you find yourselves off God's path and on a side trail, quickly confess your sin to the Lord and ask Him to put you back on His road. Since we are prone to wander off God's road, we should daily pray the prayer of Psalm 139: "Search me, O God, like a doctor examines a patient. Show me anything I need to see that isn't right and lead me back on your road."

Those who walk God's road experience His blessing. Psalm 31:19 says, "How abundant are the good things that you have stored up for those who fear you; that you bestow in the sight of all, on those who take refuge in you." Every man is hit with temptations to veer off God's road, and sometimes the hit is hard. When the temptations come, cry out to God. Run to Him. Tell Him that you are being tempted and you need Him to lead you back. When temptation hits, you may want to use some of the phrases of Psalm 142 in prayer:

With my voice I cry out to the Lord; with my voice I plead for mercy to the Lord. I pour out my complaint before him; I tell my trouble before him. When my spirit faints within me, you know my way! In the path where I walk they have hidden a trap for me. Look to the right and see: there is none who takes notice of me; no refuge remains to me; no one cares for my soul. I cry to you, O Lord; I say, "You are my refuge, my portion in the land of the living." Attend to my cry, for I am brought very low! Deliver me from my persecutors, for they are too strong for me! Bring me out of prison, that I may give thanks to your name! The righteous will surround me, for you will deal bountifully with me.

If someone were to observe your life from morning until night for a whole year, could they say of you, "There's a man who walks on God's road"? The benefits of walking on God's road are exactly what the pilgrim is searching for. He will experience Shalom. Look at the promise of verse 3 in this chapter's psalm: "You will eat the fruit of your labor; blessings and prosperity will be yours. Your wife will be like a fruitful vine within your house; your children will be like olive shoots around your table."

The rewards are clear. Your life efforts will succeed. They may not be the efforts you had in mind back in Meshek. God may change your life goals and perspectives during this pilgrimage. However, they will be very satisfying, more satisfying than anything you could have imagined before. Your relationships will be more satisfying than you ever imagined. You will no longer feel that you have to control the people around you or change them. Your wife and children will act differently.

The man who lacks Shalom experiences struggles in his home. His wife and children chafe under his attempts to force them to conform to his way of thinking. But the man who has experienced Shalom will bring peace into his home and workplace. It's amazing how this works! Unlike the discontented man who brings frustration into his world, the man of Shalom brings contentment. His wife feels protected, which is the very thing she wants. When she is surrounded by the fortification that Shalom brings, she is content to fulfill her role and she doesn't feel she has to seek protection her own way. It's the same for his children.

Some of you, at this point, may question whether people back home will be so wonderfully changed by your display of Shalom. That very question will be handled in the next chapter. For now, expect good results. It's God way. Other psalms speak of similar results. Psalm 34:9 says that the one who fears the Lord "lacks nothing." Psalm 103:17 says that his grandchildren will be righteous. Psalm 145:19 says that God fulfills their desire. These are tremendous promises. Stick with them. Don't look for something better. You'll never find it. God is on His road. Walk with Him.

The psalm concludes with the expression, "May the Lord bless you from Zion." That speaks of the source of blessing—Zion—God's presence. Zion literally means "fortification." His presence is your fortification. That expression, "May the Lord bless you from Zion," is a blessing that you can give to the other men. Encourage each other to walk God's road.

Discussion:

1. In what ways are you tempted to leave God's road for another path?

2. Commit your temptations to prayer, asking God to help you stay on His road.

3. Which phrase or phases in Psalm 142 might help you the most when hit hard with temptation to veer off God's road?

4. Have each man in the group turn to another man and speak out the blessing of verse 3: "May the Lord bless you from Zion; may you see the prosperity of Jerusalem all the days of your life."

Chapter 10

Don't Bless the Abuser

— PSALM 129 —

1 "They have greatly oppressed me from my youth," let Israel say;

2 "they have greatly oppressed me from my youth, but they have not gained the victory over me.

3 Plowmen have plowed my back and made their furrows long.

4 But the Lord is righteous; he has cut me free from the cords of the wicked."

5 May all who hate Zion be turned back in shame.

6 May they be like grass on the roof, which withers before it can grow;

7 a reaper cannot fill his hands with it, nor one who gathers fill his arms.

8 May those who pass by not say to them, "The blessing of the Lord be on you; we bless you in the name of the Lord."

The mood of our study changes with this psalm. The lesson it teaches may be difficult to receive. It has to do with abuse, with what the pilgrim's enemies have done to him and what he needs to do about it in his search for Shalom. The writer of Psalm 129 rightfully admits to being abused by others but correctly declares that there is victory over abuse. He writes in verse 2: "'They have greatly oppressed me from my youth,' let Israel say; 'they have greatly oppressed me from my youth but they have not gained the victory over me.'"

You may not feel that you are being abused in any way. However, a closer look at abuse may change your mind. Abuse comes in different forms including physical, emotional, verbal, mental, and sexual. Almost everyone experiences abuse to some degree. Perhaps the most common abuses experienced by men are emotional and verbal.

Emotional abuse comes in the form of insults, put downs, intimidation, embarrassment in public, silent treatment, or making threats. Verbal abuse can take the form of shouting, swearing, continuous arguing, interrupting, talking over you, using loud and threatening language, name calling, and mocking. Most people overlook these attacks but the one who wishes to experience Shalom will learn to gain victory over them and stop them from happening.

The abuse may come from anyone, a parent, a spouse, a boss, a neighbor, a child, or a stranger. Abuse can come at any time in life. Some people experienced abuse at school or in the neighborhood as a child. It may come in the home as a child or an adult. It may happen at work and even in the church. Abuse can even be self-inflicted as in the overuse of alcohol or drugs.

However, all abuse is destructive and must be overcome. There is also the danger of the abused becoming an abuser. Our enemy, the devil, uses abuse to keep us from experiencing Shalom. However, a man who gains the victory over abuse can not only experience Shalom but can bring it to an otherwise disruptive world.

Sometimes the process of overcoming abuse requires professional help. For the sake of this study, however, we'll look at principles taught in Psalm 129. The psalm has four parts to it—four things we need to do to address the problem and end it now. Consider each step honestly and prayerfully.

1. Acknowledge the problem.
They have greatly oppressed me . . . **(Verse 1)**

Who has or is oppressing you? It helps to name the person and admit the abuses they're inflicting. Most abused people are afraid to talk about it or they blame themselves. The abused person must own up to the situation in which he finds himself.

2. Admit the pain.
Plowmen have plowed my back and made their furrows long. **(Verse 3)**

It probably hurts to think or talk about the abuses, even if they seem small or insignificant to you now. The pain is still there. How did it feel or how does it feel? The psalmist is graphic in his description of the pain. He describes it as having someone drive a plow over his back as he lies on the ground. Some people feel it's wrong to dredge up the past or the hurts of today. However, the writer of Psalm 129 was not hesitant to decry abuse.

3. Believe that the Lord can deliver you.
But the Lord is righteous; he has cut me free from the cords of the wicked. **(Verse 4)**

God's deliverance is not based on our goodness. If that were so, then none of us would ever be delivered. It's based on His righteousness. God makes all things right. The righteousness of the Lord is the basis of our belief that He can and will deliver us from the abuses of this life. He ultimately sets all things straight. There will be no loose ends to wonder about in heaven. The enemy will come to nothing. God will see to this.

The abuser will repent and change or judgment will fall. For the one who is in Christ, judgment on every one of our sins has occurred. Christ took that judgment on Himself at the cross. For the non-believer, it will be his to pay. The abuser will either allow Christ to forgive and change him or he will face the ultimate judgment of his sinful crimes in eternity. Because of this, there is no need for vengeance on our part. We can and must forgive the abuser in order to experience Shalom. However, there is one more important step to take.

4. Set boundaries against the abuse.

May all who hate Zion be turned back in shame. May they be like grass on the roof, which withers before it can grow; a reaper cannot fill his hands with it, nor one who gathers fill his arms. May those who pass by not say to them, "The blessing of the Lord be on you; we bless you in the name of the Lord." **(Verses 5-8)**

This is where the "grass on the roof" comes in. You might be wondering what grass on the roof has to do with what we're talking about. The picture is that of a flat-roofed house, on top of which grass grew. The roots of this grass would obviously be very weak and shallow and the hot Middle Eastern sun would quickly dry out the shoots. Any grass that would grow would be short-lived and of little value. The imprecation, "May they be like grass on the roof . . ." is a desire for the abusers to be turned back in shame, in other words, their attacks would amount to nothing, just like the grass on a rooftop.

Typically, someone passing by a farmer's field would shout out a blessing to the farmer such as the one in verse 8. "The blessing of the Lord be on you; we bless you in the name of the Lord," they would say.

However, no one would be so foolish as to shout out such a blessing to someone growing grass on his rooftop.

The picture is a poignant, sarcastic, perhaps humorous illustration of how foolish it is for someone abused to call out a blessing on the one abusing him. Yet, that's basically what the abused does when he allows the abuser to continue his or her abuse and not establish boundaries. It's like saying, "Everything's alright. May the Lord bless you!" How foolish is that? So here's the lesson: Don't bless the abuser.

Learning to forgive based on the righteousness of a just God is a critical step, but it's not enough just to forgive the abuser. You must also put a stop to his or her abuse. Since God says He will ultimately put an end to abuse, we need to stand firm against it now. If God will ultimately stop it and bring judgment on abuse, it makes perfect sense that He wants us to judge it now by putting up a metaphorical hedge. A hedge is a boundary that keeps out unwanted enemies.

As much as the abused person may fear or dislike the idea that the abuser, perhaps a friend or relative, is an enemy, he or she must be seen as such in what they're doing. We can still love that person but love means helping the perpetrator overcome his or her abuse, thus freeing them and everyone else from their sinful behavior. Boundary building begins by changing the way you look at what's happening to you. They say you can't change the abuser but you can change yourself. It's true that you must bring about changes in yourself, but in doing so you just might inspire change in the other person.

Author June Hunt gives excellent advice on how to do this. Her steps are enumerated, with examples, in the article titled "How to Respond to Verbal, Emotional Abusers" available at www.christianpost. com/news/how-to-respond-to-verbal-emotional-abusers-78253/. This article is addressed to women being abused by their husbands but can effectively be applied to men abused by others.

Sometimes, abuse occurs in other relational settings, such as the workplace. Each case is different, but the steps June Hunt provides are applicable for other situations. Her four steps to setting boundaries against an abuser are:

1. Clearly state what you are willing and not willing to accept from the abuser.
2. Announce the consequences you will enforce if the abuser violates your boundaries.
3. Enforce the consequences every single time the abuse occurs.
4. Absolutely do not negotiate.

For a moment, let's look back to Chapter 9 where we learned about the rewards of walking on God's road. One reward was the emergence of good changes among those back in Meshek who experience your new way of living. We talked of how your relationships will be more satisfying than you ever imagined. You will no longer feel that you have to control the people around you, and your wife and children will act differently. Life will be better. We know, however, that some people will take a long time to change. In fact, they may choose to never change. In that event, as a man who has taken this pilgrimage and experienced Shalom, you have to exercise assertiveness and set some boundaries as described above.

It's quite possible, in looking at Psalm 129, that you realize you are an abuser. If you see any of the signs of abuse listed above, you have the opportunity now to stop and let God help you change. If you do so, it will be a great weight off your shoulders and will lead to the Shalom you seek. As an abuser, you have the opportunity to take the same four steps outlined below.

1. **Acknowledge the problem.** This is the first step to forgiveness from God and healing. Name, aloud, the kind of abuse you are inflicting on someone. Name the person or people you are

abusing. Don't put the blame for your abuse back on them. Accept it as your abuse alone.

2. **Admit the pain.** Describe the pain the receiver of your abuse is most likely feeling. Say it aloud. At the proper time and setting, admit your abuse to the one you're abusing.

3. **Believe that the Lord can deliver you.** The Lord is righteous. He will make all things right. He can do that now. Ask Him for help and then obey what He tells you, which might be to seek help from others.

4. **Put an end to the abuse.** Establish accountability to a brother in Christ or a group of brothers. Have men around you who will pray for you and exercise tough love on your behalf. You may also need to seek professional counseling. Don't delay this step. Now is the time to correct your problem so that you can continue on the road to Shalom. Instead of bringing abuse to your world, you will bring Shalom.

Not all abuse may be considered dangerous, yet all abuse is destructive. Every one of us experiences or inflicts abuse at some time. May we all prayerfully and courageously do what we can to put an end to abuse in our lives. This, in part, is the role of a man in search of Shalom.

Discussion:

1. What abusive behavior have you experienced or are you currently experiencing?
2. How have you handled it?
3. How could you handle it better?

4. In what ways do you tend to abuse others?

5. What steps will you take to stop?

Chapter 11

Confession Is Good for the Soul

— PSALM 130 —

1 Out of the depths I cry to you, Lord;

2 Lord, hear my voice. Let your ears be attentive to my cry for mercy.

3 If you, Lord, kept a record of sins, Lord, who could stand?

4 But with you there is forgiveness, so that we can, with reverence, serve you.

5 I wait for the Lord, my whole being waits, and in his word I put my hope.

6 I wait for the Lord more than watchmen wait for the morning, more than watchmen wait for the morning.

7 Israel, put your hope in the Lord, for with the Lord is unfailing love and with him is full redemption.

8 He himself will redeem Israel from all their sins.

One of the biggest barriers in our search for Shalom is personal sin. If a list of our sins were produced, it would no doubt be a long one. Even as born-again believers we still fall into sin and tend to commit the same sins over and over. Although God is always ready to forgive us, the sins we commit separate us from Him. This principle is taught in passages such as Isaiah 59:1-2, which says, "Surely the arm of the Lord is not too short to save, nor his ear too dull to hear. But your iniquities have separated you from your God; your sins have hidden his face from you, so that he will not hear."

This distancing from God can happen to any one of us if we harbor unconfessed sin. It's not that God actually leaves us. It's just that our sin hinders our fellowship with Him. God is holy and intimacy with Him is not possible when we're practicing sin. We've all experienced that feeling of remoteness from God when things aren't right between us. As we've seen, Shalom comes from being in God's presence, but when sin separates us from Him, we cannot experience Shalom. Harboring sin hinders us from bringing Shalom into our world. We must learn to deal correctly with our sins.

Let's look at the problem of sin and God's solution to it. There are at least three ways of categorizing sin: sins against God, hidden sins, and sins against others. Every sin is an affront to God. However, some can be considered as sins directed at God such as unbelief or taking His name in vain. Hidden sins are those we try to keep secret so others don't know about them, including sins of the mind and body. Then there are sins against people. Each type of sin keeps us from experiencing Shalom and bringing it into our world.

Let's consider our sins against others, such as anger, lying, dissension, neglect, selfishness, being hypercritical, controlling, demanding, or hurtful with words and actions. Any one of these could be considered abuse as was discussed in Chapter 10. They hurt others and our relationships with them. If we really want to change the way we experience life back in Meshek, we must learn to do something about our sins against people.

It's easy to be caught in a vicious cycle that begins with frustration then leads to the above-mentioned sins, which ultimately result in broken relationships and more frustration. If you're like me, you hate it when this happens. How can a man conquer this problem of sin against others? Victory begins with awareness. The starting point is to admit that we have a problem. Of course, there's often more to sins against people than what can be seen.

The above cycle of sin begins with frustration, and we need to ask ourselves *why* we get frustrated. Often, it's because we are hiding some sin. We're trying to make our relationships work while hidden sins are destroying us inwardly. That means it's time to confess. Say aloud to yourself: "I have a problem with the sin(s) of . . ." And then do the same with God. Say to Him: "God, I admit I have a problem with (name the sin) and I know it's destroying me and hurting my relationships with others.

Such confessions are what 1 John 1:9 is all about when it says: "If we confess our sins, he is faithful and just and will forgive us our sins and purify us from all unrighteousness." God invites us to admit our sin and, if we do, He says He'll forgive us. Embracing God's forgiveness helps us overcome sin. But how many times will God forgive? Two words in the above verse answer this for us: faithful and just. His forgiveness is based on His faithfulness and justice. Let's take a closer look at this concept; first, at the matter of God's justice.

To understand this, we need to go back to the cross. Jesus died in our place to satisfy the wrath of an offended God. Since God is perfectly just, He must punish sin. His justice required satisfaction and satisfaction occurred on the cross. Jesus took the punishment for our sin on Himself and thus satisfied God's justice. Therefore, God can and will forgive us any number of times because Jesus died for all our sins.

Consider these passages. 1 Peter 2:24 says of Jesus, "He himself bore our sins in his body on the cross." Isaiah 53:6 declares, "We all, like sheep, have gone astray, each of us has turned to his own way; and the Lord has laid on him the iniquity of us all." In 1 John 4:10, we read, "This is love: not that we loved God, but that he loved us and sent his son as an atoning sacrifice for our sins." Ephesians 1:7 says, "In Him we have redemption through his blood, the forgiveness of sins, in accordance with the riches of God's grace."

God took care of the condemnation brought about by our sin through Jesus. That was no small thing. Jesus agonized in the garden, pleading, "My Father, if it is possible, may this cup be taken from me. Yet not as I will, but as you will" (Matthew 26:39). He died our death that we might live.

Therefore, the basis of our forgiveness is found in the death of Jesus on the cross where He experienced separation from the Father. He knew that was coming. It was the reason He agonized in the garden. That's some heavy stuff. We shouldn't take it lightly. God will forgive us over and over even if we sin over and over. Every time we sin, God is saying, "Jesus died for that one too." So don't give up on God. He won't give up on you. That doesn't mean He's okay with your continued sin. He isn't and there is the consequence of distance from God if we persist in sin. That's when the problems at home and work set in.

Hopefully, the understanding of what Jesus went through to secure your forgiveness will keep you from sin. However, when you do fall, you should treat that sin seriously and run to God with your confession without delay. David Mains always said on his *Chapel of the Air* radio program, "Keep short accounts with God." When sin overtakes us, we should run to God immediately and admit what we've done and feel the flood of forgiveness that God brings with His restored presence.

1 John 1:9 also says that God is "faithful to forgive us our sins." To what is He faithful? He's faithful to His plan, purpose, and promises. He wants us to experience and manifest Shalom in our lives. The plan of redemption has been carried out to make that possible. Jesus cried

out on the cross, "It is finished." God accomplished it on the cross and He will forever be faithful to that plan established by His grace. God's promise in Ephesians 1:7 is this, "In him we have redemption through his blood, the forgiveness of sins, in accordance with the riches of God's grace that he lavished on us."

Confession of sin is not begging God to forgive us. Rather, it's admitting to God that we sinned. It's humbly and honestly naming our sin and accepting the forgiveness He secured through Jesus on the cross. This act of confession restores the Shalom we so desperately desire to be at peace with ourselves and others. Romans 5:1-2 says, "Therefore, since we have been justified through faith, we have peace with God through our Lord Jesus Christ, through whom we have gained access by faith into this grace in which we now stand."

Confession of sin is like a midcourse correction. It gets us back on track, more specifically, God's track. When we set things right with God through confession, our relationship with Him becomes clear again and our fellowship with Him becomes close and personal. Not only that, it restores closeness with other people in our lives. It frees us from the hidden sins that create havoc within us. With forgiveness, we can freely reach out to others as God's servants.

When we grasp the destructive nature of our sin and the havoc it brings into our world, there is every reason to run to God with our confession, seeking His help in overcoming the sin. The writer of Psalm 130 writes, "I wait for the Lord, my whole being waits, and in his word I put my hope." Come before the Lord with your sin. Admit it. Confess it. Put your hope in His Word.

Believe His promise that you are forgiven based on His justice and faithfulness. Don't say to yourself, "I'm a horrible sinner and will never be able to change the way I treat people." That's not true. It's a lie of the devil. The very fact that God forgives you when you confess is a reminder that He is working in you to bring about His plan for you. He is faithful to that plan.

Notice how the writer of Psalm 130 says it in verse 4: "With you there is forgiveness, so that we can, with reverence, serve you." Here's what he's saying: God's forgiveness restores our fellowship with Him and allows us to see how awesome He is. When this happens, we can't wait to serve Him by loving the people in our homes, neighborhoods, workplaces, and churches. We can't effectively serve Him and the people in our lives if we let sin go unconfessed. When we sincerely confess our sins to God, who loves and forgives us, we are free to focus on overcoming those sins against others with the help of His Spirit.

The last thing we need to do before moving forward is confess to others the sins we have committed against them. There's an important reason for that, as evidenced in James 5:14-16:

Is anyone among you sick? Let them call the elders of the church to pray over them and anoint them with oil in the name of the Lord. And the prayer offered in faith will make the sick person well; the Lord will raise them up. If they have sinned, they will be forgiven. Therefore confess your sins to each other and pray for each other so that you may be healed. The prayer of a righteous person is powerful and effective.

When James talks about sickness, he allows for the possibility that it might be caused by unconfessed sin. That's not true of all sickness. Not every sickness is an immediate result of one's sin. However, unconfessed sin can affect the whole person—body, mind, and soul. David writes in Psalm 32:3-4, "When I kept silent, my bones wasted away through my groaning all day long. For day and night your hand was heavy on me; my strength was sapped as in the heat of summer."

His sin left him feeling sick. We've probably all had that experience. However, there is a tremendous healing that comes to the body and soul when we go to the people in our lives and humbly confess our sins against them, not making excuses but simply admitting what we did and that it was wrong. In many cases, such action will mend a broken relationship and open the doors to wholeness of life for both you and them. That's Shalom. Even if the offended person doesn't forgive you, you will have done what is right and God will bless you for it.

Here's one note of caution: James didn't say to confess others' sins, just your own. Furthermore, you don't have to confess to the whole world, just to the one offended, although sometimes making a confession to a larger group can be a good thing. Pray and seek wise counsel about that.

Discussion:

Dedicate a period of time to confess sin. This can be done silently or aloud depending on the comfort level of the group. One group member may lead in prayer, asking God to help each man be completely honest in his confession. You may wish to go around the group having each member speak Psalm 130, verse 7 to the man next to him, using that man's name in the blank space.

(Man's name), put your hope in the Lord, for with the Lord is unfailing love and with Him is full redemption.

Chapter 12

Chapter 12

Keep It Simple

— PSALM 131 —

1 My heart is not proud, Lord, my eyes are not haughty; I do not concern myself with great matters or things too wonderful for me.

2 But I have calmed and quieted myself, I am like a weaned child with its mother; like a weaned child I am content.

3 Israel, put your hope in the Lord both now and forevermore.

The writer of Psalm 131 has learned to calm and quiet his soul—a true characteristic of one who has experienced Shalom. Imagine the difference in your life if you could do the same. You would look at your life differently and not let it upset you so much. You would be different and your life would be different because of you. The man who has learned to calm and quiet his soul is truly a happy man, but how does one learn to do this? Here's the answer in three words: "Keep it simple." That's the lesson of this chapter.

Shalom, as we've learned, is life lived the way God intended it to be lived. What makes you happy? What pursuits bring you favor and a sense of wellbeing, tranquility, fullness, and harmony? According to Psalm 131, they're not pursuits that are "great matters" or "things too

79

wonderful for me." Rather, they're pursuits that are congruent with the way God made you. When you pursue the presence of God, you have a better sense of how He wants to use you in your life.

David is the author of this psalm. He was a warrior and a king. It seems strange that he would write, "I do not concern myself with great matters." As a king, David did have great exploits. In 1 Samuel 18:7 we read that the people celebrated his victories, singing, "Saul has slain his thousands and David has slain his ten thousands." If that's not greatness, what is?

What is David talking about in this psalm? He's certainly not calling himself lazy or minimizing his role as king. He simply knew his calling and fulfilled it with the gifts God gave him, and with much prayer in the power of God. God made David with gifts that suited the role of king. For someone else, being king would have been beyond their gifting, but for David, "king" was a perfect fit.

It wasn't in the avoidance of his responsibilities that David found Shalom. It was by attending to his responsibilities that he found Shalom, without looking somewhere else for greatness. The "things too great for me" refer to things not of his calling but another's. God had gifted and chosen him to be a warrior and king, nothing else. David didn't try to become something he was not chosen to be. He worked hard in his area of giftedness in a role for which God had chosen him. I'm sure that brought him a great feeling of satisfaction.

What causes a man to leave his area of giftedness and attempt pursuits that he's not fit for? The opening line of Psalm 131 gives the answer: pride. It's thinking that we have the ability to do anything we choose to do. It's the lie of our culture that says, "You can do anything you put your mind to." You probably know people who have followed that advice and are experiencing stress because of it. In verse 1, David writes: "My heart is not proud, Lord, my eyes are not haughty; I do not concern myself with great matters or things too wonderful for me."

David knew God had made him a certain way and he applied himself to the things that worked well for him. He never tried to be a priest. Saul did and got into trouble (See 1 Samuel 13). Uzziah also tried that and got into trouble when he offered incense on the altar (2 Chronicles 26:16). The point of this chapter is that you can learn to quiet your soul by sticking to what you were called and equipped to do. Do it heartily and in cooperation with the Holy Spirit within you. Enjoy it. Give yourself fully to it. This is how you "keep it simple."

The man who has learned to calm and quiet his soul is a man who lives his life to the full, the way God has created him. He knows his gifts and talents and he uses them the way God intended him to use them. He's not lured away by something that's beyond him simply because it offers a bigger salary, glamorous office, or an important title. These things aren't wrong as long as they fit the giftedness God has placed in you.

Simply put, the first verse of Psalm 131 says, "I don't try to be something I'm not made to be and I don't try to do something I'm not gifted to accomplish." Satan tried that. It's called sinful pride.

Satan, also called Lucifer, is the ultimate example of pride. We read of his prideful desires in Isaiah 14:12-15:

How you are fallen from heaven, O Lucifer, son of the morning! How you are cut down to the ground, you who weakened the nations! For you have said in your heart: "I will ascend into heaven, I will exalt my throne above the stars of God; I will also sit on the mount of the congregation on the farthest sides of the north; I will ascend above the heights of the clouds, I will be like the Most High." Yet you shall be brought down to Sheol, to the lowest depths of the Pit.

Satan had everything going for him as a servant of Almighty God, but he lost it all because of his foolish pride. The following passage tells his sad story:

You were the seal of perfection, full of wisdom and perfect in beauty. You were in Eden, the garden of God; every precious stone adorned you: carnelian, chrysolite and emerald, topaz, onyx and jasper, lapis lazuli, turquoise and beryl. Your settings and mountings were made of gold; on the day you were created they were prepared. You were anointed as a guardian cherub, for so I ordained you. You were on the holy mount of God; you walked among the fiery stones. You were blameless in your ways from the day you were created till wickedness was found in you. Through your widespread trade you were filled with violence, and you sinned. So I drove you in disgrace from the mount of God, and I expelled you, guardian cherub, from among the fiery stones. Your heart became proud on account of your beauty, and you corrupted your wisdom because of your splendor.
Ezekiel 28:12-17

God has made us the way we are and when we cooperate with the way He has made us, we find contentment. When we, in pride, decide that we can do something better, we are setting ourselves up for a fall. Be who God has made you to be.

When you know what you're called to do and you do it, you find great contentment. David says he was like a child who has been weaned. Before weaning, a child cries and whines until he's fed. Once he's weaned, he knows he will be fed and patiently waits for it. In the same way, we need to learn to stick to our calling from God and wait on Him for the strength and wisdom to diligently carry out our daily responsibilities. When we try to do what we're not gifted at or called to do, we might end up whining. The Interpreter's Bible explains it this way:

What has brought about this change (this "weaning")? Has he become stoically resigned to life's defeats? Has he given up the struggle because of old age or weariness? No! . . . Like the merchantman in the New Testament seeking goodly pearls, and who discovered at length the "pearl of great price," he has come through many discouragements to find in God, rather than in things, life's highest satisfaction. So, come what may, he rests in the Lord and trusts in him for the issue.

Vol. IV, page 683

Whether you're currently holding down a job or you're retired, try to find ways to use your gift more in what you do. Change what you do or the way you do it to accommodate your giftedness. The more you serve in the way you're gifted, the more content you will be. The more you seek God for help in doing this, the more you will experience Shalom. The psalm ends with the instruction to put your hope in the Lord. The implication is "keep it simple."

Discussion:

1. How has God gifted you?
2. How can a person recognize his giftedness?
3. What are you doing now that is not fully utilizing your giftedness?
4. How can you modify what you're doing to maximize your giftedness?
5. What can you do differently to "keep it simple"?

Chapter 13

God's Plan Is Bigger and Better Than Yours

— PSALM 132 —

1 Lord, remember David and all his self-denial.

2 He swore an oath to the Lord, he made a vow to the Mighty One of Jacob:

3 "I will not enter my house or go to my bed,

4 I will allow no sleep to my eyes or slumber to my eyelids,

5 till I find a place for the Lord, a dwelling for the Mighty One of Jacob."

6 We heard it in Ephrathah, we came upon it in the fields of Jaar:

7 "Let us go to his dwelling place, let us worship at his footstool, saying,

8 'Arise, Lord, and come to your resting place, you and the ark of your might.

9 May your priests be clothed with your righteousness; may your faithful people sing for joy.'"

10 For the sake of your servant David, do not reject your anointed one.

11 The Lord swore an oath to David, a sure oath he will not revoke: "One of your own descendants I will place on your throne.

12 If your sons keep my covenant and the statutes I teach them, then their sons will sit on your throne for ever and ever."

13 For the Lord has chosen Zion, he has desired it for his dwelling, saying,

14 "This is my resting place for ever and ever; here I will sit enthroned, for I have desired it.

15 I will bless her with abundant provisions; her poor I will satisfy with food.

16 I will clothe her priests with salvation, and her faithful people will ever sing for joy.

17 Here I will make a horn grow for David and set up a lamp for my anointed one.

18 I will clothe his enemies with shame, but his head will be adorned with a radiant crown."

The message of the previous psalm, Psalm 131, was to be content with how God has gifted you in life and not attempt to do something you're not equipped for. Be active and constructive, but within your calling and gifting. Once you're content with who you are and what you do best, you can find great calmness and quietness of soul as well as great joy by working hard at that calling.

David was called to be a king and he worked hard at it. He had many ambitions, one of which was to build a dwelling place where the people could meet with God. He was passionate about this goal. The first line of Psalm 132 speaks of how David's passion led to his self-denial. David was willing to set aside his own needs in order to accomplish this work for God. We can be like this too. We come up with a project to please

God or our wife or family and we relentlessly pursue it. However, as this psalm teaches, God's plan is bigger and better than our plan, and sometimes our wife's is too.

Let's examine this more closely. We're almost done with this pilgrimage. There have been many lessons along the way. Each one has helped us understand and experience Shalom. It's easy for us to think, "I know what I'm doing. I've learned many lessons. I will now go back to Meshek and make things work." That's the I-can-fix-it attitude. If we go back to the places in our lives with that attitude, we'll create more harm than good.

The point of this pilgrimage is to experience change in ourselves so that we can live the life of Shalom—to be blessed and to bless others. If we return with the goal of changing others, it won't work. If we go back thinking that we now know how to bring Shalom to our world, we will be very disappointed with the results. Only God can bring Shalom to our world. Our role is to go back as changed men, men who have learned the lessons of Shalom, and to simply let the changes be evident in our attitudes and actions.

Psalm 132 looks back on a time when King David was resolved to build a dwelling place for God. It was a passion of his. He longed for a place where he and the people of Israel could go to be in the presence of God. However, God had chosen David's son to build His dwelling place. Solomon would build the temple. The historical context for this psalm is found in 1 Chronicles 17:1-15:

After David was settled in his palace, he said to Nathan the prophet, "Here I am, living in a house of cedar, while the ark of the covenant of the Lord is under a tent." Nathan replied to David, "Whatever you have in mind, do it, for God is with you." But that night the word of God came to Nathan, saying: "Go and tell my servant David, 'This is what the Lord says: You are not the one to build me a house to dwell in. I have not dwelt in a house from the day I brought Israel up out of Egypt to this day. I have moved from one tent site to another, from one dwelling place to another. Wherever I have moved with all the Israelites, did I ever say to any of their leaders whom I commanded to shepherd my people, "Why have you not built me a house of cedar?"'

"Now then, tell my servant David, 'This is what the Lord Almighty says: I took you from the pasture, from tending the flock, and appointed you ruler over my people Israel. I have been with you wherever you have gone, and I have cut off all your enemies from before you. Now I will make your name like the names of the greatest men on earth. And I will provide a place for my people Israel and will plant them so that they can have a home of their own and no longer be disturbed. Wicked people will not oppress them anymore, as they did at the beginning and have done ever since the time I appointed leaders over my people Israel. I will also subdue all your enemies. I declare to you that the Lord will build a house for you: When your days are over and you go to be with your ancestors, I will raise up your offspring to succeed you, one of your own sons, and I will establish his kingdom. He is the one who will build a house for me, and I will establish his throne forever. I will be his father, and he will be my son. I will never take my love away from him, as I took it away from your predecessor. I will set him over my house and my kingdom forever; his throne will be established forever.'" Nathan reported to David all the words of this entire revelation.

God's message was that He had a bigger and better plan than David's. God would build a house for Himself and He would use Solomon, David's son, to accomplish it. There's a hint in this message that God is speaking of more than just Solomon. He says, "I will be his father and he will be my son." This is a reference to the coming Messiah, Jesus the Christ. Therefore, we can see that God's plan was much bigger and more far-reaching than David could have comprehended.

We men can easily miss God's bigger and better plan by impetuously jumping into our own plans. Sometimes a wife tells her husband about an idea she has for making improvements to their house, and the husband thinks, "I know what to do!" Then, without waiting to really understand her thoughts, he jumps in and makes the changes he thinks she'll like. Instead of being patient and listening, the husband moves ahead without her, which says to her, "I know what you'll like better than you do." How does that make her feel? What's more important to her: for you to fix the problem, or to listen and understand what she needs? How much more important, then, is it to listen to God before "launching" His plan?

Many of us would love to do great things for the Lord. However, our ideas may be too soon, too small, or quite different than what the Lord has in mind. An important lesson for the pilgrim is to patiently seek the Lord and His will. Listen to Him and others. God will have a role for us to play back in Meshek in His bigger and better plan. It may be a role different than we expected, but it will be His role for us. David's role was to prepare the way for the building of the temple by clearing the land of God's enemies. In the process of winning battles, David took spoils from the enemies he defeated and those spoils became resources that Solomon used to build the temple (See 2 Samuel 8). David's role was crucial, and so is yours.

Don't get too fired up with passion and plans for changing things back home. Focus on the changes God is making in you even now. Be passionate about that. God will make the changes in your life in His timing and in His way. His plan is bigger and better than yours, and you will have a significant part in that plan. Let Him work His plan in your life and follow Him in doing it. Your part in God's plan may be different than you think, but it will be very significant and rewarding.

Discussion:

1. Talk about a plan you've launched that was too soon, too small, or too different than what God or your family had in mind.
2. In what ways has God been changing you on this pilgrimage?
3. How will those changes make things better back in Meshek?

Chapter 14

Unity Is the
Sweetness of Life

— PSALM 133 —

1 How good and pleasant it is when God's people live together in unity!

2 It is like precious oil poured on the head, running down on the beard, running down on Aaron's beard, down on the collar of his robe.

3 It is as if the dew of Hermon were falling on Mount Zion. For there the Lord bestows his blessing, even life forevermore.

Along with the writer of Psalm 120, we made the choice to withdraw from our old, frustrating, unsatisfactory life in Meshek and take this pilgrimage in search of Shalom. Soon, we will return to Meshek having learned the lessons of Shalom and face life at home with a different attitude, with different responses to problems, and with the goal of, not just being transformed, but seeing our world transformed.

Although the pilgrimage is almost over, there's one more stop we need to make. It's the City of Zion—the destination of our search. However, before we get there (Chapter 15) we must learn one more lesson. It's the lesson of unity. When we arrive back in Meshek, we'll be different than the person we were when we started this journey. However, it often happens that when one person changes for the better, those back in Meshek react negatively toward them, which creates disunity and more problems.

Either they think the returned pilgrim is trying to act better-than-thou or that this new persona is just a temporary fad that won't last. They're skeptical. Be prepared. It could happen to you. If you're given such a reception, don't become frustrated and angry. Don't withdraw and give up or try to force your new way of living on them. That would be unfortunate to say the least. You don't want to create more disunity. What should you do, then? The answer is found in Ephesians 4:1-3: "I urge you to live a life worthy of the calling you have received. Be completely humble and gentle; be patient, bearing with one another in love. Make every effort to keep the unity of the Spirit through the bond of peace."

Be completely humble and gentle with those back home. Don't tell them about your new way of living, just live it. Let them observe it until they see that it's for real. Your example, not your words, will win them over and draw them into a closer relationship with you and with the God of Shalom. God will bring about unity "through the bond of peace." He will create oneness through the presence of Shalom.

If we're at peace and not uptight, angry, or reactive, then those around us will be at peace as well. Remember the words of Proverbs 15:1, "A gentle answer turns away wrath, but a harsh word stirs up anger." If we take the lead in getting upset and angry, others will follow suit. But if we let God direct our words and actions, it will create an atmosphere of

Shalom. Remember the signals from Chapter 4? The good servant will sense God's signals and respond accordingly.

In some cases, others may, at first, be so skeptical they'll make life more miserable for you than before you left Meshek. But what they're doing is testing the veracity of your new life. If this happens, be patient, humble, and gentle and watch what God eventually does in their lives. There may come a time when you can share with words what happened to you. However, be aware that some people in your life may never accept the new you. If the negativity persists, you may have to set boundaries. (See Chapter 10 for a discussion of boundaries.) In any case, keep living the lessons you've learned and let the Shalom of God fill your life.

Don't let the enthusiasm for your new life turn others away. Let God create a close unity by simply living the life of Shalom. God has given you Shalom in response to the lessons he's taught you along the way. Now use that Shalom to draw people to you and God and not drive them away. They will need time to learn the same lessons you've learned, and your example will be instructive to them.

The imagery of Psalm 133 helps us learn the lesson of unity. The psalm says that unity is both good and pleasant. The Hebrew word for good used here is Tob, meaning beautiful, delightful, or precious in quality. It was used seven times in the Genesis account of creation where God looked at what He made and said it was good (Tob).

The word translated as "pleasant" is Nā`īm. It means sweet, used elsewhere in the Old Testament for the taste of bread and the music of the lyre. Unity is the sweetness of life. What a great description of what we long for at home!

How can we get this sweet unity? We certainly don't create it by our efforts. The psalm makes it clear that it comes down from God. All the imagery of Psalm 133 points to Him as the source. Notice the repetition of the word "down" and the reference to "falling." This sweetness of life comes down from God, not up from us—so don't force it on others.

We have to let God bring down that sweetness. Don't get in His way. Don't destroy it with impatience or pride. Remember the lesson of Chapter 7? Some sacrifice may be required. It might be a great sacrifice. The people in your life may never change but you can remain changed and experience the blessings of Shalom. Recall the words of Jesus in the Garden of Gethsemane, when he faced the challenge of the cross. He said, "Not my will but yours." Those were words of submission to the Father. Jesus put God the Father first even before His own desires and comfort. We must do the same.

We're not saying to other people, "I will submit my will to yours." We're saying those words of submission to God the Father. We're to do what He says, not what others say. If we submit to others, it should be because God says so. In so doing, we're letting Him do His work through us. Don't get in the way. Practice saying, "Not my will, Father, but yours." Be patient, humble, and gentle. Practice all the lessons you've learned along the way. Review them. Renew them when you slip and fall. Be humble and ask God and others for forgiveness. Reach out in love to others in your life, as a servant of Christ. Simply stated, put God and His will at the center of your life.

In his excellent book, *Disappearing Church*, Mark Sayers talks about how St. Benedict sought to change his culture and bring it back from selfishness to God-centeredness. Sayers writes "St. Benedict understood that to rebuild a culture . . . one had to return Christ to the center." Our goal is similar. We want to return to Meshek as changed men who will turn the culture of our homes, churches, and workplaces into places characterized by Shalom. To get there, we must place God at the center of our lives by saying, believing, and living the not-my-will-but-yours attitude.

We are God's servants, not here to carry out our own will but the will of our Master Jesus. When we are tempted to react negatively to people in our lives, we must pay attention to the prompting of the Spirit, or as we learned in Chapter 4, watch for His signals and obey them. If He prompts you to stop, then stop before you react to a difficult situation. If He prompts you to take action, do so, but always with the attitude of "not my will but yours." What would God have you do, say, not do, or not say? Follow His signals.

By acting this way, your life will be sanctified or set apart by God as a place in which He will bring down His Shalom. Psalm 133 pictures precious oil poured on the head of the priest, flowing down over his beard and robe. The act of pouring oil on the head of the priest was a sanctifying action setting him apart for God's special work among the people. When you live the not-my-will-but-yours lifestyle before God, He pours over you the sanctifying oil of His Spirit, setting you apart to be a priest in your world. You have been set apart (sanctified) to experience Shalom and to bring it into your life.

Oil is also a symbol of prosperity and blessing. (See Deuteronomy 32:13; 33:24; Psalm 92:10.) Scriptures refer to it as "the oil of joy" (Isaiah 61:3; Psalm 45:7). There it is—Shalom: favor, prosperity, safety, wellbeing, tranquility, fullness, harmony within and without, restored relationships, and vigor and vitality in all dimensions of life.

You're about to return to Meshek. As you apply the lessons of this pilgrimage, you should never again have to say, "Woe to me that I dwell in Meshek." You have been transformed. Now go back and allow God to transform Meshek. But first, we have one more stop—the City of Zion.

Discussion:

1. Talk about frustrating situations back in Meshek that could have been handled differently with the not-my-will-but-yours attitude.

2. Talk about a difficult situation back in Meshek that could have resulted in disunity but didn't because of your willingness to let God work through you.

Chapter 15

Bringing It Home

— PSALM 134 —

*1 Praise the Lord, all you servants of the Lord who minister
by night in the house of the Lord.*
2 Lift up your hands in the sanctuary and praise the Lord.
*3 May the Lord bless you from Zion, he who is the Maker of
heaven and earth.*

The pilgrim of Psalm 120 has arrived at his destination, Zion, the City of God. However, it's night. One would expect a joyful daytime entry after such a long journey. "Why night?" you may ask, but there's a lesson here. As the pilgrim enters a dark city, lit only by the burning lamps of the temple, he sees only the night workers. What do night shift workers do? They do the dirty work. They clean up the messes made by the daily sacrifices and make preparation for the daytime staff. There's nothing glamorous about this job.

Life back in Meshek is filled with messes too. Like the night shift workers in Zion, we have some cleaning up to do back home. Some of the messes back there were created by us and some by others, but we, with God at the center of our lives, are the ones to clean them up. It's a rugged service. It will take sacrifice on our part. There's nothing

97

glamorous about it. But God is with and in us. We've been set apart for this work. It's a holy, sanctified work.

Could it be that if we cease to tightly grasp at our own desires, stop defending ourselves and give ourselves for others as Christ gave Himself for us, that God would give us back our world in a new way? Consider these verses:

For whoever would save his life will lose it, but whoever loses his life for my sake will find it. (**Matthew 16:25**)

Blessed are the meek for they inherit the earth. (**Matthew 5:5**)

The meek will inherit the land and enjoy peace and prosperity. (**Psalm 37:11**)

That's Shalom! Isn't it interesting that those who want everything lose what they have and those who are willing to let it all go get everything? The picture of meekness is not weakness, but coming before God with an open hand. Try this. Hold out your hand with a clenched fist. Inside that fist you hold all the things you feel you deserve to keep: your possessions, your time, your rights, and your pride. Nothing is getting out, but nothing is getting in either.

Now open your fist and stretch out an open hand, palm up. That represents meekness. You're not giving up anything, yet. All the things you treasure are still in the palm of your hand. However, you are making it all available to God. He's welcome to take away anything He wants, but He can also put into your hand anything He wants to put there. That was not true of the man with the clenched fist. Which man, do you think, will experience Shalom?

I don't know what's waiting for you back in Meshek, however, I know this: it's okay to work the night shift in God's house as long as you have the presence of God with you. Even those who ministered at night in the City of God did so with a heart and mouth filled with praise to the Lord.

Are you ready to go back to Meshek?

"May the Lord bless you from Zion, he who is the Maker of heaven and earth."

Discussion:
1. Review all the lessons taught on this pilgrimage.
2. What lessons have been most helpful?
3. In what ways have you already changed from the person you were at the beginning?
4. Where do you still need the most help?
5. What will be your next steps?

About the Author

ROY HANSCHKE understands the needs of men and how
to effectively communicate principles from God's Word that
help them succeed in a society bent on discouraging, if not
destroying, them. His job in Christian radio (KPOF Denver) allows
him to hear men's stories, meet with pastors, pray with men at their
businesses, and speak to them in churches and church men's groups. He
knows how hard it is to be the influence most Christian men want to be
in their world.

Roy trained for ministry at Moody Bible Institute, Trinity College
(Deerfield, Illinois), and Trinity Evangelical Divinity School, where
he received degrees in Biblical Studies and Religious Education. Roy
received additional training from the school of hard knocks in church

pastoral ministry, commercial real estate, on the staff of a government agency, and by running his own speaker training business.

Roy's published writings include youth materials for Success With Youth Publishing Company (1970s), articles in *The Toastmaster*, *Quiet Waters Compass*, *Mobile Beat* (cover article), and CHEC Homeschool Update. He also has a published story in *Heart-Stirring Stories of Love* (Linda Evans Shepherd, Broadman & Holman, 2000).

Roy loves reading, sharing daily devotionals on his morning radio show, teaching speaker workshops, ministering to neighbors, and hiking in the mountains of Colorado. He and his wife live in Centennial, Colorado, near their three children and sixteen grandchildren, and attend Foothills Bible Church (since 2004).

Morgan James
Speakers Group

We connect Morgan James published
authors with live and online events
and audiences who will benefit
from their expertise.

Morgan James makes all of our titles available
through the Library for All Charity Organization.

www.LibraryForAll.org